Fight Doctor

FERDIE PACHECO, M.D.

SIMON AND SCHUSTER · NEW YORK

DESIGNED BY EVE METZ
MANUFACTURED IN THE UNITED STATES OF AMERICA

1 2 3 4 5 6 7 8 9 10
LIBRARY OF CONGRESS CATALOGING IN PUBLICATION DATA
PACHECO, FERDIE.
    FIGHT DOCTOR.
    1. MUHAMMAD ALI, 1942–   2. BOXERS (SPORTS)—
UNITED STATES—BIOGRAPHY.   3. PACHECO, FERDIE.
4. PHYSICIANS—FLORIDA—MIAMI—BIOGRAPHY.   5. SPORTS
MEDICINE.   I.   TITLE.
GV1132.M84P3   796.8'3'0924 [B]   77-7064
ISBN 0–671–22894–3

TO ANGELO AND CHRIS DUNDEE, WITHOUT WHOSE HELP AND FRIENDSHIP I WOULD NOT HAVE EXPERIENCED THE CRAZY WORLD OF BOXING.

TO MY WIFE, LUISITA, AND CHILDREN, DAWN, FERDIE AND TINA, WHO HAVE BROUGHT SUNSHINE, JOY AND PURPOSE TO MY LIFE.

Contents

CONTENTS

Introduction

I call Dr. Pacheco my Playboy Doctor because he's always going to all the big fights and lives in a big house, paints pictures, and has nice cars, but he is really my boxing doctor. That is something he really knows something about— fighters.

My trainer, Angelo Dundee, first took me to see Doc when I was starting out in Miami. See, Dr. Pacheco has a little office in the heart of the ghetto and he is the onliest white man that is down there helping poor people and the fighters.

He helped me when I hadn't even had but a few pro fights, and he would never take anything for it. He never would charge *any* fighter no money, and still doesn't to this day. That's why I like him, we both like to help people who need it. Of course today, after I got to be the Heavyweight Champion of the World, I do pay him, even though he never once asked for a dime.

Dr. Pacheco has always helped me in my fight career. He took care of my cracked rib with Quarry in Atlanta, he arranged everything in San Diego when Norton broke my jaw, and all during my comeback he had to treat my hands so I could punch without them hurting. He has worked in my corner since the first Liston fight and I like to have him

9

there. It's nice to know you got a doctor that knows fighters and fight medicine. Doc sure knows about that 'cause he been taking care of the Dundee fighters for years.

I'm glad to see Doc do a book about boxing. It just goes to prove what I been saying: "If you stick with me long enough, I'll make you all famous."

Dr. Pacheco is many thing to many people, but most important to me, he's My Friend.

MUHAMMAD ALI

PART ONE

Inside the Ropes

1·Tales of the Fifth Street Gym

The last perfect example of a boxing gym is located above the drugstore at the corner of Washington Avenue and Fifth Street in the South Beach ghetto of Miami Beach.

Stillman's Gym in New York, you say? Long gone. Gleason's Gym? Still there, but no contest. There simply are no boxing gyms today alive with action except for the Fifth Street Gym. Action in the form of fighters in all stages of their careers preparing for action, every one getting ready to step into harm's way.

Gym activity depends on fight activity. In Miami Beach we are fortunate enough to have the last dynamo of boxing promoters, Chris Dundee, whom age cannot wither, nor can custom stale his infinite variety of fight cards built from zero talent. He develops fight cards with what he has, and he builds local fighters into international attractions. For better than twenty-five years Chris Dundee has patched together fight cards, fought, cajoled, blackmailed, threatened, conned, connived, and convinced fighters to fight for him for short bread. The result is that he has had some truly great fight nights in Miami Beach. He has also had some mediocre ones, and some real "smellos," but mainly he has had *fights*, and that is why the Fifth Street Gym is alive and well.

The Fifth Street Gym looks like it was built as a set for

a bad boxing movie. First it is up a flight of stairs, over the drugstore. The stairs alone are worth the trip if you are a student of decay and of what can be done by several generations of termites. The stairway is lit by a solitary bulb of brilliant fifteen-watt variety. The light can hardly be described as blinding. The entranceway is guarded by a gnome. The price of admission is fifty cents and this comprises part of his salary, so he is more than alert at letting the "mud turtles" and free loaders into the wondrous gym.

There are literally thousands of stories about this guardian, Emmet (the Great) Sullivan—Sully to his friends. He is a refugee of the cold and harsh life of the New York jungle. He is stooped over and virtually toothless. His clothes hang on him like Caesar's toga hung on him after several senators took their best shot. His lifeless cigar is pushed to the corner of his mouth, and a brown dribble of tobacco-laden saliva courses down his withered jowl into his brown stained collar.

Sully's main preoccupation is that someone will sneak by him without paying the tab of four bits. *Esquire* writer Wilfred Sheed, assigned to do the text on a picture book on Ali, tried to get by him by airily murmuring, "Press."

"Yeah, press your pants. . . . Come up with the four bits, mud turtle." Sully would not relent. Faced with so formidable an adversary, Wilfred capitulated and coughed up the four bits, which is another first for the Fifth Street Gym Hall of Fame.

When things are tough and it is hard to come up with a cornerman Sully works the corner, but some fighters are loath to have Sully in the corner because of his annoying habit of keeping the cigar in his mouth during the fight. Jerry Powers, the Prince of Second Avenue, a veteran of over three hundred fights, was struggling through a dreary four rounder when he suddenly quit in the corner. Amazed that he quit, I sought him out in the dressing room and asked him why. "Oh, Man, the old dude kept burning my shoulder with the cigar every time he reached for the water."

Once past Sully you are safe for the moment. The place is large, but seems small from the amount of people in some type of frenetic physical activity. Two walls are lined with dirty windows, in the middle of which some long-since-forgotten da Vinci has painted a pair of boxing gloves and the word GYM in yellow on a red background. The walls are also peeling and fading, but the effect is just perfect. The floor is in the same state of advanced decay as the stairs, but having been worn by the rub of millions of leather-bound shuffling feet pounding away at the hypnotic rhythmical ritual of rope jumping, it is patched hither and thither with slabs of plywood. Some years a weak attempt is made at repairing and painting the floor, but the paint is sucked in by the dry wood, and the plywood wears out faster than the hardwood, and in no time the pharmacist below is in danger of being floored by a falling heavyweight.

There is a rope extending from Sully's table at the entrance to the square ring used for sparring sessions. To the left of this are some wooden benches for spectators, seldom used unless Ali or some name fighter is in town. In the near corner the desk of Chris Dundee, with a cracked glass table top and a phone with a dial lock on it. Chris, well aware of the propensity of the fight crowd for long-distance calls, has long ago obviated the problem by locking the dial. He solves incoming calls in other ways.

Chris received one long-distance call through the operator, collect. Chris feigned deafness and the operator spoke again to the in-calling party, who persisted. Again Chris couldn't hear. "The connection is bad, honey," he said in his sweetest tone.

The voice on the other end is frantic. "I can hear *him,* operator, tell him I need five hundred bucks today to bail out of a jam. Urgent."

"I can't hear a thing, operator." Chris again, trying to hang up.

The operator, exasperated by the bantering back and forth, finally speaks to Chris. "I can hear him perfectly well, Mr. Dundee. He says he needs five hundred dollars."

"If you can hear him, honey, *you* loan him the five hundred," Chris says, hangs up, and makes for the stairs before the phone rings again.

By contrast, Chris' brother, Angelo Dundee, may be the softest touch in all of boxing. Angelo still has one old fighter borrowing money who has not fought in five years, nor will he ever fight again. Once every month he labors up the dark flight of stairs at the Fifth Street Gym, dons his fighting togs, and reels around the floor in a pathetic pantomime of a boxer training for a bout. At the end of this sad exhibition, he touches Angelo for the monthly loan. Angelo is now down more than ten thousand dollars to this man. So much for the typical picture of the bloodthirsty trainer who is still sucking money from a finished fighter.

Watching his new Bahamian champion Elisha Obed train is the venerable Moe Fleischer, who is still very active in helping Chris make matches and train fighters. Moe says he is approaching 75, but he doesn't say from which end. He has a heart condition, but is alive today because Chris the Godfather rescued him from the killing boredom of retirement and put him to work in boxing. Moe flourishes in the gym, is active, useful, and a bright spot for all fighters. He has a gentle touch, a kidding way, and a lovable way of sending out preliminary kids to take solid beatings. He is an old-time cornerman, which translates into a man that won't let his fighter quit, a man that will do anything to win a fight. Moe, like all the old dinosaurs of the gym, dwells on past triumphs, and past associations with champions. In Moe's case his champion was Kid Chocolate from Cuba. No one compares to Chocolate in Moe's eyes, and the most he can aspire for his new champion, Elisha Obed, is that he reach the shoetops of Chocolate. Moe dwells with rapture on the old days, but his main coups were scored as a highly successful promoter in New York. Here he was given the sobriquet Sellout Moe, a name that seems rather ambiguous in meaning, but which he is proud of nonetheless. Sellout Moe rode high in the hurly-burly days of boxing and is a fountainhead of old boxing promotion stories, the best of which I never tire of telling when things get dull on the after-dinner talk circuit. Here is one.

Sam Aranson ran a hustling emporium in Williamsburg, Brooklyn, and had fighters to send to all parts of the country during the thirties when the Depression made boxing a haven for the hungry. He had sent a fighter to fight in Boston for Eddie Mack, but the fighter got hurt the day that the match was to take place.

With very little time to keep the card together, Eddie phoned Sam. "Sam, you gotta help me. The heavyweight fell out. Get me anybody . . . *please.*"

"Eddie, how good an opponent you got?"

"A black boy, not bad, banger, can't take a punch, no heart."

"Eddie, I got a great-looking kid, Jewish, heavyweight, 200 after training today, ready . . . fourteen straight knockouts!"

Silence on the other end of the line. It sounds like Eddie is crying. You must understand that a white, Jewish heavyweight with fourteen straight knockouts in New York City is an annuity for life in the thirties. There are a million black guys ready to fight but the Jewish heavyweights are usually at the cashier's window, settling up after a fight, not in the ring. To offer this wonderful kid on a day's notice is an act of the highest kind of brotherly love.

"Sam, this kid with the fourteen KOs . . . you would send me this kid? What do you want, a mortgage to my gym for the kid?"

"Five hundred and expenses—send me my end straight."

"Sam, I promise I won't get this kid hurt. . . . Put him on the next train, I will personally meet the train . . . and Sam, I'll add a few bucks in gratitude. You have saved my life . . . the kid can fight here any time you want . . . Thanks Sam, thanks."

"Skip the thanks, send the money."

That night in Boston there is a sellout crowd. The word goes through Beantown that a great young Jewish heavyweight, fourteen knockouts, is fighting Battling Bummer. The first round is all action, and the young kid is killing his opponent. The second round is more of the same but the embattled black swings from the floor and catches the Jewish heavyweight on the jaw. Down he goes. The crowd is on its feet.

"Now he's in for it, he made our guy mad with that slip. . . . Boy, oh boy, is he going to hand it out now."

But slowly the crowd grows silent, for the count is past eight and then nine and finally the fateful ten, and still no sign of life from the prostrate Jewish juggernaut. Down and counted out.

Back in New York the next day at the gym, Sam is waiting for the results. No phone call. He busies himself with the affairs of the day and along about three in the afternoon the phone rings and a crestfallen voice on the other end identifies himself as Eddie from Boston. Sam almost yells into the phone, "Did you send my money?" First things first in boxing.

"Yes, I sent it with the kid. He left an hour ago; he will get there pretty soon."

"Good, good. And, say, how did the kid do?"

"Well, Sam, the first round was dynamite. What a jab that kid of yours has got, and nifty footwork too. The first round he win big."

"Cut the blow-by-blow . . . what happened?"

Resignedly, Eddie decides to tell it like it is.

"Sam, the kid gets knocked out in the second round. . . . Jeez, I'm sorry, but . . ."

"Fifteen straight knockouts!" says Sam, and hangs up.

This is the Fifth Street Gym and its people. This is where, many years ago, my association with Muhammad Ali began.

2·The Kid—Cassius Clay

Angelo called to say he was sending a new kid over for a cold shot. He also said that this was the new kid they were high on, and to treat him extra nice. As I was hanging up, a young giant walked into the office and began a nonstop monologue that lasted fifteen years.

My initial impression of Cassius Clay was that he was very nervous and covering up his anxiety with whistling-in-the-graveyard type of talk. He was certainly a superb specimen, he was certainly handsome, and he really could talk. Now if he could only fight.

At the start of his career Cassius Clay was handled by the Louisville group, a group of well-meaning, well-intentioned sportsmen who had taken a liking to Clay, the 1960 Olympic Medal winner, and aimed to guide his career and invest some of his funds so that at the end of his boxing life he might have a few hundred thousand to show for his efforts. The mind boggles at the comparative financial results for Clay if he had remained with them, but again, life plays funny tricks. Had he remained with them he would have gone to Vietnam. He most certainly would not have ended up a worldwide figure, adored beyond belief in countries throughout the world and enshrined by the youth of the sixties and early seventies as a cult figure. Then again, since all investments went sour in the mid-seventies, he might have seen his life savings washed away in the market and other "safe" investments. Who can tell what Cassius Clay would have been if he had stayed with the Louisville group?

Certainly he would not have the stature of Muhammad Ali, and what white establishment group would have had the temerity to ask for, and get, millions for the one-night services of Muhammad Ali or would have risked the title in faroff lands like Africa, Indonesia, Malaysia, and the Philippines? I am afraid the staid, establishment-oriented Louisville group would have stuck to the form and continued to fight in the Astrodome, the L.A. Colosseum, and, for the really big fights, Madison Square Garden. They would unquestionably have gloated over having gouged the Garden a million for his services.

But on this quiet day in my office in the central Miami Negro ghetto, Ali was still Cassius Clay, and he was mainly intent on talking me out of giving him a needle and into giving him oral medication. Through the fifteen years since then he has taken hundreds of needles from me, but he has changed little in his dislike of the injection as a form of therapy. Unfortunately, if understandably, the brotherhood of boxers is one united by a common bond of pain, and Clay had not yet become adjusted to it. In the end, as we will see, he surprised the fistic world with his ability to take pain in order to persevere and win. But that was in the future and that day, in my treatment room, we did a slow bullfight Veronica turn: I was the matador and he was the bull. He twisted and turned and I was caught up in the comic faena until finally I lunged and injected him. The mocking laugh I was to know well in the future years echoed in my office, along with a shy "You sumptin else, Doc; didn't feel a thing."

He knew I was going to the gym, and I gave him a ride in my new Cadillac. He was busy talking about cars and what he was going to do when he won the title. Some kid, I thought, hasn't gotten started yet and he's talking about what cars he is going to own, and what he is going to do with the money.

Cassius Clay had been sent to Angelo Dundee to train and this meant moving out of Louisville into the Miami Beach Fifth Street Gym and, for lack of better housing, into a ghetto hotel on Second Avenue. At the time I had an established charity practice in the ghetto, which was so active that I had to cut down my office hours for whites to accommodate the patients.

It was a hellhole of pimps, hookers, drug dealers, winos, and general bad guys. Into this abscess came the innocent boy athlete, Cassius Clay, and because of his gregarious nature, size, and accomplishments, he was adopted by the hustlers and protected. He was easy to like and no one would quite take his braggadocio seriously, but looking at that fine torso, they couldn't totally disbelieve either. Now that hotel was totally committed to gratifying the senses and desires of anyone of the human species. Cassius studied these forms like he did everything else, his puton sense of humor acting as a buffer both for his innocence and his sense of destiny.

At this stage of his career he had adopted a spartan-like attitude and held that his body was his future and his destiny as the heavyweight-champion-to-be of this world. His one ambition was to be the heavyweight champion and he had not deviated from it since he had run alongside the school bus, while the other children rode in its warm comfort, yelling at the kids making fun of him:

"I'M CASSIUS CLAY. . . . I'M GOING TO BE THE HEAVYWEIGHT CHAMPION OF THE WORLD."

I respectfully submit that few of us know what we want to be at the age of 12, and especially something contingent on one's future size and weight, but Clay was as sure as he could be of anything. His mother, a sweet lady known as Odessa, said at this early date that this was all Clay thought about morning, noon, and night, and it was still overpoweringly true at the age of 19 in Miami.

At night they would entice him down the street to the liveliest cabaret this side of Harlem, the Sir John, and there, in the company of some of the sleaziest characters in the ghetto, Clay would groove on the night life, and Sin City never could exceed the excesses of all things evil and sinful he witnessed there. In time, as we will see, this played a great part in his decision to become a Muslim, one of the decisions which enabled him to fulfill his destiny. He would sit quietly sipping an orange juice, and no one forced him to have any booze, and no one suggested drugs to him, for he was protected by the hustlers themselves and they took a pride in him. Sissies passed him by admiringly. Beautiful, long-legged, full-bottomed black ladies strutted by with their pimps, and if they hesitated the man would say, "Naw, man, he is fighting next week in L.A. What you trying to do, man, hurt our man?"

At a reasonable hour, he would get up and walk the two blocks to his hellhole room and pass the night by himself. Never again in his boxing life would he have such will power. Later, when the ladies were always available for Ali wherever he would go, he would always accommodate them —but not now, not in his youth. He was a crusader on a solemn Crusade. He was after the Holy Grail. He was pure and he would remain so until he conquered the Saracens and obtained the Holy Grail. Then, and only then, would he become human.

At dawn he would get up and do roadwork on Biscayne Boulevard, in front of the residential area I live in, Bay Point. While he ran, I slept, and while I began my day in my office, he slept; then we both would go to the gym at midday, but by different routes. I would get in my air-conditioned Cadillac and cruise over the MacArthur Causeway, sometimes passing the young Cassius Clay, running with a sort of racehorse beauty in his heavy work boots. He would wave and smile, and I would know better than to stop for it was his way of doing even more roadwork, and I would think, *That is going to be some tough nut for Sonny to crack.*

By this time, Cassius Clay was something of a story in the sports pages. What exactly was he? A nut, a buffoon, a charlatan, a braggart? All this and more was asked. Hard writers could not believe his con. What was that bullshit about calling the round? Gorgeous George has come to boxing, they said, and, if the truth were known, they were partially right for the kid had talked to Gorgeous George in Las Vegas and formed the bulk of his "act" around what the popular wrestler said. He wore white shoes. He bragged outrageously. He predicted. He acted sophomoric. He outraged the boxing establishment. He followed Gorgeous George's act but improved on it. Gorgeous George was in show business, with a beginning, middle, and finish to his wrestling act, but Ali was ad-libbing, winging it when he stepped into a boxing ring. There was no script. He could fall on his ass and it was all over. He had to produce, and produce he did. The first part of his career is like a montage of one of those old Warner Brothers biographies with pages of the calendar flying over railroad tracks whizzing by, and names of his opponents floating by in sports page headlines. And the Ali train was on the way.

However, en route to the title, two things happened that almost caused the Clay Express to derail. One was the Henry Cooper fight in England. The other was the Doug Jones fight in the Garden.

England, with its tolerance for eccentrics, took Clay to its heart. Clay loved it and reveled in the attention. However, he was Clay the Rude when they stepped into Wembly

Stadium that day: Clay had devised a paper crown and robe to wear into the ring. Surely he meant to imply that he was the uncrowned heavyweight king but the English, always sensitive to jokes about the Royal Family, took it the other way, and loud were the hoots of derision when Clay stepped into the ring. Ole 'Enery was snorting, and although the prospect of losing his usual few pints of blood was excellent, he could not wait to apply his crunching left hook to Clay's jaw. The fight went as predicted: Clay danced and Cooper bled, and Clay was waiting until the predicted round to knock out Ole 'Enery and, as a result, got careless, and Ole 'Enery let fly his devastating hook which caught Clay just right, and he went down onto the last strand of the ropes. As Clay was getting up, the bell rang, saving him from a British victory greater than El Alamein. In the corner, Angelo, ever the alert cornerman, was working with feverish intensity when, lo and behold, he espied a tear in his man's glove. Instantly, he pointed this out to the British officials, who immediately sent their minions scurrying thither and yon to find another suitable pair of boxing gloves to permit the contest to continue. When, one might ask, was the last time a glove tore in British history? The last time a glove tore was when Henry the Eighth tried to jam his fist down the throat of Catherine of Aragon. Nevertheless, Ole 'Enery stood by, a picture of futility, as the seconds ticked by and the young stallion across the ring gathered his strength and cleared his head, and, finally, a glove was found, and Ole 'Enery soon had the distinct impression that this glove fit his chin well, and that long before he passed out from loss of blood he would pass out from a surfeit of leather. And so it happened, and the Clay Express rolled on toward the mountainous Sonny Liston.

Doug Jones was another milestone, but for another reason. True, the fight was hard and the decision close and, to some nonbelievers, wrong, but the main thing that this fight netted him was Bundini. Drew (Bundini) Brown, the hysterical pilot light behind the Clay shenanigans, the witch doctor, the black source of strength and faith, the irascible, lovable con artist, the faithful follower, the irreverent troublemaker, friend and enemy, Iago, rogue. He was at one time or another all these things but Cassius Clay took him to heart as a soulmate. Here was a man who understood his blackness and the black humor and the puton and the need to exult in prefight high jinks. And through all his faults, quirks, drawbacks, and embarrassments, he was there as a mysterious source of strength for Cassius Clay. And so, for better or worse, he had Drew Bundini Brown in his corner, and no man ever had a more fervent believer. He believed, my god, how he believed! Undoubtedly his street smarts saw the Kid as a likely vehicle to fame and fortune, but aside from his immediate view of the Kid as a passport out of the oblivion of the ghetto, he truly believed in his future as a great man. Not just in boxing but as a national figure and, maybe, if the Establishment didn't squelch him, as an international figure. For better or worse, the Kid adopted Bundini and, aside from a few excommunications, Bundini was by his side in all his big fights. And so the little caravan of the faithful began to increase to its eventual wagon-train size, and Cassius Clay rolled along toward the big test, a rendezvous with the apparently unbeatable Sonny Liston.

3· Training and Corner Work

I have often been asked to describe what a young fighter must go through to prepare himself for fight night, what happens in the corner during a fight, and what happens after the fight. I have never read any detailed description of this process, so I will try to give you one.

A fighter usually trains for a big match from four to six weeks, but many fighters get little warning of when they are fighting, so they have to remain on a more or less continuous alert. Big-name fighters and champions rest between fights. An aging one takes longer to get in shape than a youngster, but all fighters should maintain their roadwork even if not training actively. Work on the road is the cross most fighters have to bear to keep their legs in the condition that they need. Legs are the key to a fighter. Let us, then, start with roadwork.

When a fighter is in his teens, his legs are his strongest asset. However, as he gets older, constant attention must be paid to the legs, for this part of the anatomy is the easiest to fall into disrepair. "The legs go first" is an axiom of boxing. The fighter knows that his legs are crucial in taking him to the opponent in the chase, or in eluding him, and in the balance so necessary for punching power, as well as in stamina. Two main methods of keeping the legs in condition are daily roadwork, and jumping rope when in training.

The fighter usually gets up in the predawn hours and picks a park, racetrack, or lonely stretch of road that suits him. Some fighters prefer grass, others a paved surface. Some have tried loose beach sand, but that seems to be the worst thing a fighter can run on, forcing the legs to struggle too hard and thus defeating the purpose of roadwork.

The time-honored hour to run is at dawn, but just why remains a mystery. The best legs I ever saw on a fighter were those of Luis Manuel Rodriguez, the Cuban welterweight champion, and he preferred to run at six in the evening when the sun was going down, and before his evening meal. It seemed infinitely more sensible than upsetting your sleep at dawn, but old customs die hard, and every other boxer I know runs at dawn.

The distance a fighter runs is determined by his trainer, and in the later stages of his career, by his own judgment. It depends on his needs at the time. Most good fighters can run five miles a day, but as a rule don't. The average is a good three miles. Too much running is like too much training and is likely to result in overtiredness—a hard lesson to teach young, eager fighters and inexperienced overambitious managers and trainers. Too much hard work can kill a fighter's stamina almost as thoroughly as not enough work. There is a fine line between the two, and it is mainly a judgment call by the trainer. Therefore, experienced trainers like Dundee, Clancey, Futch, Sarria, and Ferrara are worth their weight in gold.

The fighters usually run forward at a jog, although some alternate running hard, then jogging, then running hard. Some whose boxing lives depend on leg speed also run like cornerbacks in football, backward for a stretch, then forward, then backward again. This is very wise because they are building up strength in the muscles they will use in retreat, as well as in the attack. Willie Pastrano hated roadwork as much as any man ever did, but his remarkable career depended on his legs and he did not neglect his roadwork. Muhammad Ali does his roadwork religiously, and it has kept him on top for a long time. I could cite many a fighter who fell by the wayside because he neglected the road, but let bygones be bygones.

Following roadwork, the fighter usually goes back to bed, after drinking some tea or juice. He gets up again around eleven o'clock in the morning and goes to the gym to put in about two hours of work. We will skip the instruction phase of a fighter's career because I am talking about professional fighters here, and not amateurs or fighters in the making.

He dons his gym togs, which are basically like the ones he wears in a fight, and begins by loosening up. Every gym has a bell which times three minutes, and some trainers carry their own watches to time training phases by three-minute rounds. When the fighter is warmed up, he begins the five phases of his training in the order prescribed by his trainer. He usually starts by skipping rope, punching the light bag, then the heavy bag, spars a few rounds, and then does his exercises.

Skipping rope is the necessary adjunct to roadwork, and it develops the resistance of the legs to fatigue. There are as many ways to jump rope as there are fighters. Again, the "fancy dan" fighters skip rope in an artistic fashion, while the plodders skip rope in a plodding fashion. Sugar Ray Robinson made rope skipping a show business number. Willie (Pep) Pastrano, Douglas Valliant, and Luis Rodriguez skipped rope beautifully and with a light touch. Liston skipped rope heavily to the leadened beat of a slow blues record, "Night Train." Surprisingly, Ali is rather unimaginative in his rope skipping, but he does not neglect it at all, whereas he sometimes skips the heavy bag.

Punching the light bag helps the fighter's speed and reflexes. Hitting the rhythmically bobbing light bag develops timing, accuracy, speed, and reflexes. He might keep at this for two, three, or four rounds, depending on his needs. The fighter's arms are always up in a raised position, since the bag is at head level, and this develops the muscular ability of the arms to be kept raised during a fight.

Punching the heavy bag develops punching power and stamina. This huge, heavy bag hangs by a chain suspended at body level and the fighter pounds it as it sways back and forth. Many fighters work differently with the heavy bag. Luis Rodriguez and Willie Pastrano, not known for their punching power, did a beautiful dance with the bag, letting it sway to and fro, ducking under it, punching it as it passed away from them, and occasionally digging in a hard body punch as it came to them. Watching these two master boxers punch a heavy bag was a thing of beauty. Watching Sonny Liston and George Foreman punch a heavy bag was like watching a man get mugged. The trainer would hold the bag rigid and the fighters would pummel the bag with sledgehammer blows. At times, you would swear you could hear the bag grunt as it got hit. Muhammad Ali would punch the heavy bag in a combination of these two disparate styles, letting the bag sway and playing with it in his artistic style, then leveling hard punches at it when he felt time in each round was about up. Later in his career, it became apparent that much of his hand trouble was attributable to his punching the heavy bag. As he adopted the easier way of punching the heavy bag, his hands got better and better. Now, if you watch Ali train, you will see him flick the heavy bag instead of socking his hands into it.

Sparring while in training is a very important element in

preparing a fighter. There are various factors of great importance. The main one is to choose a sparring partner who will best simulate the style of your fighter's opponent and/or a sparring partner who will permit your fighter to work on his best moves and so sharpen his tools to a fine edge. Very often trainers get whoever is available in the gym, without regard to these factors, resulting in "gym wars" which are no good for either fighter and contribute to an early retirement. Philadelphia fighters are known for their gym wars, and they seem to wear out faster than most fighters, coming into bouts in a generally stale condition. The fighter that got the most mileage out of this type of training is Joe Frazier. However, I feel that he has paid the price for these wars in rapidly deteriorating health. Ali has had a long career because he goes "easy" in the sparring department. He knows what he can do in the ring, and does not need sharpening like so many other fighters do. The single most difficult thing for a trainer to evaluate is when a boxer has had enough sparring and is getting stale. Some fighters spar until the day of the weigh-in. Others lay off a few days before the fight. In the "I-saw-it-but-I-don't-believe-it" department, I would have to class Ali's nonstop, no-rest fifteen rounds of sparring the *day before* the Bugner fight in Malaysia as the most remarkable and foolish thing I have ever seen.

Most neglected of the five training steps is the exercise phase. There are several reasons for this. First, the fighters hate the gruelling, painful process; second, most trainers don't know the proper exercises; and, third, it comes at the end of the day's training when most fighters are tired and would like to go to the showers and get something cool to drink. Of the most talented trainers I have seen, one stands out above the rest, and he is Luis Sarria, a demon at the exercise table. He trained all the great Cuban fighters, and they were always known for their great stamina and speed.

His masterpiece is Muhammad Ali, and he is merciless in the training room, away from the show biz of training Ali, and Ali shows his true grit as a champion who knows that there are no short cuts to body conditioning. Ali pays the price, but his reward is greatness. Only a superbly trained Ali could have pulled out the third Frazier fight, with an outstanding display of stamina, when everyone thought he was exhausted and beaten. He won that fight in the training room. Sarria had him ready to fight.

The exercises themselves are designed to strengthen the neck musculature, as well as the abdominal and back musculature. We have seen that the arms and legs are taken care of in the gym and on the road. One does not want to interfere with that indefinable something called "punching power," which has nothing to do with bulky muscles. In fact, the more muscular a fellow is, the less he seems able to punch hard and long. One of the heaviest punchers I saw was a skinny Cuban kid named Douglas Valliant, who has absolutely skinny arms, but could hit you with the force of a cannonball. Muscle building of the type that is produced by weight lifting and exercise is absolutely contraindicated in boxers. The exercises that Sarria prescribes gives the body strength and ability to take punishment. Neck and abdominal musculature must be strong to resist punches, and yet the body must be supple, not rigid and boardlike, because a boxer must have mobility and flexibility, and he must duck and bob and weave. Sarria's method allows a boxer to be all of these things and yet take a great body shot without visible effect. It certainly has worked well with Muhammad Ali, hasn't it?

A fighter leaves the gym and usually devours a meal of steak and salad, with a large natural fruit juice drink. If he is not trying to make weight, he may eat again at night. He holds off on all fattening foods, no sweets, no alcohol. It is a monotonous diet, but all fighters seem to tolerate it well. Following a fight, they eat as they please until the next training session starts. The subject of the proper weight for the fighter varies from trainer to trainer, because as the fighter grows older he changes in weight, and if he isn't already a heavyweight he soon is in the next division having to cope with fighters of larger anatomical dimensions. The lumps get bigger. So usually a trainer likes to keep his fighter at his best lowest weight, which results in some agonizing years for fighters who are natural welterweights trying to fight as lightweights years after they can make that weight naturally. The results are sometimes disastrous. As a fighter grows into the next division, he may find that physically he cannot take on the bigger guys and he is faced with three choices: go back to his lower weight at the cost of agonizing weight watching; resign himself to fighting physically bigger guys and taking bigger beatings; or retire. Weight is a bugaboo that has destroyed many a good fighter. The most spectacular change I witnessed was Jimmy Ellis going from middleweight to light-heavy to heavyweight in a year's span. Although he got to the point where he fought at 200 pounds, Jimmy was never a genuine heavyweight, and you have but to see him next to a full heavyweight like Ali, Liston, Foreman, or Frazier to understand what I mean.

The fighter must get his rest, and that is not usually a problem with a well-trained fighter. However, the usual factors enter into this. Is he married? Does he have small children? Is he single? Does he chase girls? Does he live with a girl? The fighter has all of the problems that normal people have, and then some. He is often in dire economic straits. He has to abstain for a few weeks from sexual activities. He has to have a special diet. He has to be in bed early, and get up at dawn. He has to be able to sleep late after he gets back. Unless he is in a training camp, as few fighters are, one can see how disruptive this training schedule is to a family. He leads a solitary life while training. No one can help him, no one can share it but another fighter, and that is the solution many fighters take. Champions are forever sharing their time either with doting managers or sparring partners who share their suffering and schedule. Rest becomes a factor, and lack of it can be a killer. Angelo had a fighter who was pure murder in Miami, but when he went to the Garden he got Gardenitis, which is a virulent form of disease that strikes young fighters going to New York for the first time. The fighter, Sugar Cliff, could not sleep three days before the fight. I dared not give him sedatives because of the adverse effect on his reflexes. He was a zombie when he walked into the Garden that night, and he fought like one.

Regarding sexual mores and superstitions, I will just briefly touch on this controversial aspect of boxing. Sexual activity is a normal, human function. It can in no way be debilitating if done prudently and in a reasonable fashion. By that I mean that it would be suicidal to take on three ladies on the day of the fight, but to have intercourse a few days before a fight is not, per se, debilitating. If this were so, many a great fighter would have bitten the dust, including some super champions. What it *does* do is rub some of the aggression (known as *the edge*) off a fighter. Abstinence causes aggression. Fighters get mad and mean, and that is the name of the game. Most fighters need this to be at their best. Super fighters like Ali do not: he is seldom mad at an opponent, and given his talent for boxing scientifically, he does not need angry emotion; he needs cool detachment, which Ali has plenty of, lord knows. The other factor involved is also psychological. A fighter thinks he is *ready* if he has paid the price of abstaining, and conversely, is fearful if he has fallen by the bedside, and since he has repeatedly been told what a weakening effect this has on a fighter, he believes it. When he does engage in intercourse

before a fight, he feels the weight of his guilt-ridden conscience, and it affects his performance. I do not differentiate
between oral sex and intercourse since the end result is, or
should be, the same: a healthy orgasm.

The men who work a fighter's corner can win a fight for
him (infrequently), help him in a supportive sense (always),
and sometimes lose a fight for him (not so infrequently).
They literally have the power of life or death over a fighter.
Well, let's look at a corner, what happens there, step by step
in the fight, and how it can be of utmost importance to the
fighter and the fight. Let's also look at the men who work
there in anonymity most of the time.

A typical fight corner is made up of the chief second, who
is usually the manager-trainer, and two helpers to handle
the chores of carrying the buckets and stool into and out of
the corner. There are two buckets. One is for receiving the
waste products of the fight: spit, blood, and excess water. The
main bucket is half filled with ice, a taped quart bottle of
water, vaseline, a sponge to rub down the fighter, and an
ice bag to keep swelling down initially, then to revive the
fighter later in the match.

The main cornerman is carrying the cut stuff if he is, as
in most cases, also the cut man. Cut stuff is usually a thick
cement-like paste made up in a variety of ways. He also has
an adrenalin bottle (topical), a powder (bismuth subgal-
late), which also acts as a firmer for the paste, and an
anticoagulant. In the old days, ferric chloride was permitted,
and it was called dynamite, which it most certainly was. It
caused a caustic burn in the tissue and stopped the flow of
blood, but because of inadequate medical facilities to treat
the cut properly after the fight, it caused irreparable harm to
the tissues and was outlawed. The cut man carries an assortment of poppers, which are either the old smelling salts,

35

aromatic spirits of ammonia, or any nitrate. He also has some Q-Tips with added cotton wrapped around the ends for stopping nosebleeds.

The fighter is checked to see that he has his mouth protector (mouthpiece) in, his protective cup in place, and, incidentally, his trunks on. Many a fighter has taken off his robe to find that he has neglected to put on his trunks, much to his dismay and to the merriment of the audience. In the dressing room before the fight, the fighter has had his hands wrapped by the chief second. This is a widely divergent ritual in most dressing rooms. The trainer starts with gauze bandages and wraps the hands, round and round, until he has used all the roll, coming to the fingers and back as far as the wrist. Then a roll of tape is placed on top of this. In England they barely put any tape on, and none of the round-and-round type, but cut strips and place them over the gauze. They do not seem to get more hand fractures than we do, but that does not change our way, and Americans wrap round and round until the hand appears encased in a solid wrapping. The gloves are then put on in the dressing room or, in special fights, in the corner within view of the audience. A cornerman from the other corner usually views the wrapping and glovings as a precaution that no hanky-panky is going on, such as loading a glove with plaster of Paris or a horseshoe.

The fighter and the three cornermen are then brought into the arena and go through the ritual of introductions and prefight ceremonies. The fighters touch gloves and the fight is ready to begin. The first round is usually a slow round with both fighters feeling each other out. There are times when the men fight the hardest in the first round when they are fresh, and many of these end in first-round knockouts; but usually the first round is a feel-out round. Now the fighter returns to his corner. The work starts.

A good corner usually has one main man doing the talking

between rounds. Other cornermen discuss the fight as it progresses in the corner, while the fight is taking place, and may reiterate what the main man has said or offer minimal encouragement, but the chief second does the real talking. As the fighter comes to the corner the stool is waiting for him, and he sits, usually instinctively with his arms up on the middle strand of rope. The chief second takes his arms off the ropes and makes him sit with his gloves between his legs so that the arms receive the maximum amount of blood. The second wipes off the perspiration with a cool sponge, removes the mouthpiece, and hands it to another cornerman who refreshes it with water. He may or may not give the fighter a rinse with water. He takes a minimal amount of vaseline and wipes the fighter's eyebrows with this grease to make them slick and stop any possibility of a cut, or at least to diminish it. This process is repeated through the fight, but it varies with how things are going.

If the fighter is cut, the corner begins to earn its pay. The chief second, or cut man, relegates his other duties to his assistants and begins to take care of the cut only. This is done in the following manner, with variations by each cut man, of course. As soon as the boxer sits down, the cut man cleans off his face with the towel and presses the edges of the cut together for at least ten seconds. Pressure stops more cuts than do medications. Then, depending on what type of cut has been inflicted, the cut man uses the various medications at his disposal, saving the stronger ones for the last. The English do not permit any cut medicine stronger than topical adrenalin, which is truly amazing, because they achieve remarkable results. Joe Bugner, fighting Muhammad Ali in Vegas, sustained a cut almost immediately, but his corner did such a job that, in spite of the fact that it took eight sutures to close it, it was never a factor in the fight. Americans put considerably more medications in the cut, and therefore require more specialized care after the fight, which usually is not available. More on that in a minute. Back to the cut.

After the medication, the trainer tries to squeeze the cut as tightly as he can to exert pressure and to squeeze the medication into the end arteries that are bleeding. Usually a few punches on these tissues and they reopen; however, a good cut man can control most cuts very well, and a great cut man like Angelo Dundee can save a title and possibly millions of dollars. Mantequilla Napoles failed to call Angelo to work a fight in Syracuse against Billy Backus, and it cost him the title when the fight was stopped because of a cut. Had Angelo been there, Napoles would not have lost the title that night. Good cut men are hard to find, but when one comes along, everybody should hang onto him. There are many butchers around who pass for cornermen and cut men, but that is due to the absence of licensing, training, and the brutal nature of the sport and the men it attracts.

The balance of a fight is a battle against exhaustion, and a good corner team works at an escalating pace to forestall the ravages of exhaustion. The corner begins to refresh with more and more water, cool and soothing to the back and neck, massage to the arms and legs (in the final stages), ice-bags to the neck, and finally, as a last resort, the contents of an ice bag into the protective cup. Such a procedure netted me a chagrined look from a comic, bright young fighter I was working with named Frankie Otero. He was exhausted as he came back for the ninth-round rest, and as he arose I poured the icy content down the front of his body into the cup. He looked startled and, as he went to meet his foe, he turned to me and said, "Was that absolutely necessary, Doc?"

The most important job of the chief second is to know when to call it a day and end the fight. Life and death sometimes hang in the balance, and at the very least, further punishment can be averted and the fighter's career and tissues can be saved. The dying off of the old cornermen, so praised in the old literature, and the coming to age of good, sensible, judicious men have contributed to a change in attitude toward cornermen. In the old days, a cornerman who stopped a fight prematurely would be out of the business for life, forever suspect, and accused of that most dread of boxing afflictions: "being soft." The legendary cornermen of the twenties and thirties were very hard house men. Their allegiance was to the management, not to the fighter. A fighter was supposed to keep going until hc could not stand or see, thereby creating the image of the old punch-drunk fighter.

Nowadays, it is quite unusual to find punch-drunk wrecks. The boxing commissions oversee fighters better, not permitting them to fight with regularity if they are getting knocked out often, and not permitting them to fight at all after a knockout for a specified length of time. The physical examinations are sharper. Some states insist on an electro-encephalogram. The fighters' careers are shorter now, both in years and number of fights. An old-time pug would reach one hundred fights in no time, since he fought almost weekly, and he'd keep it up until he was wheeled away. The new breed may not have fifty fights in a career spanning eight or nine years.

The new cornerman has a new criterion. He is guided by more humane impulses. He is a friend of the fighter, not the house. His duty and obligation are to his fighter and his fighter alone. He is not encumbered by other responsibilities and is backed up by the press and the public, who have also become more humane in the last twenty years. They no longer call for blood. The image of poor Benny Paret hanging on the ropes is etched in the minds of the millions who were a witness to that moment. Now, when a fighter is taking a whipping and looks like he has no chance to make a fight of it, the corner steps in, or the referee steps in, and stops the bout. Probably the single best line at a press conference to illustrate the judgment of a cornerman was uttered by Angelo Dundee, who had stopped the Ellis-Frazier title match in the Garden after Ellis had been down twice in the preceding round. Ellis was asked which of the two knockdowns was the worst for him. He answered, "I wasn't down twice, he only knocked me down once." After which Angelo addressed the reporters: "See what I mean?" This was conclusive proof that Angelo had done the right thing. Another example of corner judgment and bravery was the Eddie Futch decision to stop Joe Frazier from answering the bell for the fifteenth round in Manila. Joe was ready to come out but Eddie, in spite of thinking they were ahead, would not let Joe go out to receive the punishment that awaited him. In the old days, he would have been taken over the coals by his peers and by the press. But that day, happily, he was cheered by the press and congratulated by his peers.

Unfortunately such uniformity of excellence as is seen in the work of experienced cornermen like Eddie Futch, Angelo Dundee, Chickie Ferrara, Luis Sarria, Ray Arcel, Bill Gore, and a few lesser names and foreign cornermen is not encountered routinely in areas less than championship and contender circles. They are the exception rather than the rule, but why is this the case? The reasons are fairly simple, so let me say them simply:

1. *Lack of proper training grounds.* Boxing is dying. No young people are trying to get into it because it does not seem to have a bright future. The old boys are not anxious to teach young dogs their tricks. There are no teaching grounds, and no one is in a hurry to develop any. Each man has his secrets and they are his stock, which he shrouds in mystery and mumbo-jumbo.

2. *Lack of financial remuneration.* Cornermen are terribly underpaid. Even the manager and trainer are not well paid, and as far as that goes, the boxer isn't getting rich either.

One must get to championship caliber before the game begins to pay off, and long before then the little guys have been gobbled up by the big guys. You have to do boxing as a sideline or hobby to be interested in cornerwork or training fighters and, even then, be thick-skinned enough to stand the insults and deprecations of the older cornermen. No one is as good as "us old guys," and young men are run off at a fairly regular rate.

3. *Lack of proper licensing.* Anybody can work in a corner. Anybody. There are no restrictions except morals clauses, and I can't tell you how ineffectual that is in keeping ex-cons and hard guys out of corners. As far as I am concerned, a strict rule should be made to prohibit the *relatives* of fighters in corners. Their judgment is impaired, naturally, but strangely enough, usually in the wrong direction. Sensing a slur to the family honor, a father keeps his son fighting long after he should quit, and brothers are even worse. Prominent ex-fighters do not seem to have good corner judgment. This is usually because they can see things that *they* could have done as champions, but their charges cannot do them. Great fighters like Ray Robinson, Joe Louis, Archie Moore, Willie Pep, Saddler, and the like do not make great cornermen. Theirs is a different drummer. They have tasted glory and grandeur, they cannot be in supportive roles, they cannot tolerate shortcomings that they did not possess. The best cornermen fought very little or *never fought at all.*

The medical aspects of working a fight are also rather simple. I prepare a fighter by letting the trainer do all the work, and not interfering unless there is an acute problem of medical nature. I do not feel you can substitute drugs for roadwork and gym work. There are no mysterious potions, vitamins or elixirs that one should give a fighter before a fight. He is, after all, in the prime of life—a hale and hearty young man. How can you improve on nature?

During a fight, I work as one of the assistants to Angelo Dundee, and this aspect is where the pleasure in boxing comes in for me, since I am actively involved in running a fight corner and running a fight. If Angelo is not working, I work as the chief second, or help if the chief second is a man like Luis Sarria. If Angelo is not in the corner, I do the cut work. If Angelo works, I help him. You cannot improve on perfection.

After a fight is when I earn my keep. Unusual as it may seem, there are no dispensaries or surgeries in any fight arena I have ever been to. This creates an immense problem because, unbeknownst to the public, a doctor from another city or country is not allowed in any hospital other than his own, which means that if I have a fighter severely injured in New York, I must seek a doctor who has privileges in a New York City hospital, and admit the patient through him. This creates complications, so I usually take a full plastic surgery kit with me and operate in the very dressing room at the arena or in the hotel room. Contrary to every known theory, including germ theory, I have not had one wound infection in fifteen years of sewing up fighters in the filthiest of surroundings. I know not why.

As soon as the fight is over, I scrub the dressing table and lay the fighter down while, as the saying goes, his blood is still hot. I then scrub out all the accumulated goop that we have put in the cut, and prepare to débride the area. Before this is done I inject novocaine, so that I can work without causing the fighter further pain and can be assured of a quiet, still patient. It is well to note here that the English do not allow anything but adrenalin, so that all of this is not necessary for their fighters; all things considered, this is a very sound thing. They also do not feel that the use of a local anesthetic is indicated, and on that point I disagree. It is a small thing to inject a small amount of novocaine, and I feel that the fighter has been through enough pain for one night. There are no contraindications to it, and I do not feel that the "stiff upper lip" attitude should be asked of a fighter following a match.

The actual work cannot start until every particle of foreign substance is cut out, and the edges of the laceration evened with a scalpel. Then and only then can the suturing begin. The sutures I use are the thinnest made, and are placed very close together with a very small "bite" so that the cut is closed as tight as if one had sewed a zipper in place. They seldom reopen in the same spot.

Why, then, do boxers have that lumpy, furrowed brow tissue? This is because there is a shortage of doctors who like boxing enough to devote some time to it. It is certainly not lucrative. I work for nothing. The man normally in charge of such repair is the commission doctor, but that job is usually filled by a chap who enjoys watching the fight and disappears shortly thereafter. I do not refer to cities like New York and London, which have fights often, and employ commission doctors who love boxing and are in continuous action. The majority of fights are in smaller towns which have fights infrequently, so that the doctor does his disappearing act almost as soon as the fight ends.

The promoter faced with an unwanted addition to his overhead also disappears, or sends the hapless boxer to a public hospital emergency room. Here he is taken care of by an intern who is just getting his practice suturing cuts. That's hardly the way to treat a man whose future may depend on the type of suturing job you do. The burden of payment now falls on the poor manager, or the boxer, since there is almost no type of insurance to cover the boxer's medical bills. In cities where there is a minimal medical insurance, the promoter is loath to let the boxer use it since it will result in raised rates. It seems a vicious cycle, but the one who ultimately pays is the poor boxer who has gotten his lumps, is hurt and bleeding, and is trying to hang onto his rapidly disappearing purse.

Schemes have been presented to obviate this form of abuse, but none seem to work. There is also always a plan contemplated to provide for a fighter's retirement, in the form of a small percentage removed from each fighter's purse for a retirement fund. However, the nature of boxing and the lack of organization itself makes this unlikely ever to be adopted. Let's face it, boxing is an anachronism, a holdover from other, tougher days, a highly individualistic sport, and it does not lend itself to administrative organizations of a benevolent nature, such as can be instituted in profitable team sports like football or basketball.

To return to medical problems, injuries of a more serious nature occur now and then, and must be taken care of at the time of injury. Fractures and neurological problems are the most common injuries that spring to mind. Both require the use of a hospital, and it is always well to strike up a good acquaintance with a doctor in the town before you get there, in order to use his hospital privileges. Fractures are usually of the hand or jaw, and occasionally of the cheekbone, or zygomatic arch. Most require surgery then and there, and that is another king-size headache. Again the fighter must pay, and few are the smaller fighters who can afford the price of the hospital. I can impose on my friends in plastic surgery and orthopedics to do these operations free, but no hospital will turn out to be that charitable.

Fractures of the hand are more delicate and susceptible to refracture. Jaw fractures *hardly ever* refracture. I have seen but one elbow fracture, and a lot of rib fractures, but these are inconvenient more than career ending.

Neurological injuries are very serious and all have to be treated as if they are life threatening until proven otherwise. They require hospitalization and specialized diagnosis and care. The same cost problems arise, and the same lack of solutions is offered.

I have been asked many times what a solution to this would be, and frankly I do not know. The more I am familiar with the economics of boxing, the more I realize how hard it would be to come to a solution. The presence of a trained boxing doctor in each corner would be nice, but impractical. Where can you find that many nutty doctors? Who is willing to leave a busy practice to work in every type of fight in any city under abysmal conditions at no recompense? Only a few dyed-in-the-wool boxing freaks could be found in the entire U.S.A. Yet we need people interested in helping the boxers if boxing is to survive. We need the involvement of good people at all levels. Boxing is not just Muhammad Ali in all his glory. It is the little guy on a small fight card, in a four-round preliminary in a dive. It is a fight in the back, blackest part of a Caribbean island.

The last step, then, is to retire the fighter. When is he through? "The fighter is the last to know" is the saying at the gym. How true. I have seen fighters, intelligent, former champions, half blind and on their way to full blindness, plead for one more fight. I have seen proud men with enviable records ruin them by fighting years after they should have retired. How can that be? Is it a question of an unscrupulous fight manager or promoter? No, though Hollywood movies would have you believe that. The fault generally lies with the fighter. He cannot believe he is through, even after several beatings should have convinced him. He will not accept it, and he plods doggedly on. The boxing commissions are helping with this problem now, but they have to tread gingerly in this minefield. Lawsuits can emanate from this, and everyone involved moves cautiously because it is hard to prove objectively what you know subjectively. "That guy is shot," you hear an old boxing guy say, and you can usually make book on it, but try to prove it in court.

So, in the absence of guys with real moral fortitude, the fighter continues, and his end is predictable. Since I am not involved financially, I am more direct with a fighter and can tell him he is through when I think he is through. I refuse to work with him again, and I will not even attend his fights. If it is a question of provable damage, as in the case of a fighter going blind, I will go directly to the boxing commission, lay the evidence before them, and let them take the action, if need be. Some fighters stop talking to you, but in the end, years later, they always come back and say the same thing. "You were right, Doc. It was time to quit. Thanks for leveling with me."

PART TWO

Muhammad Ali— Champion and Champion in Exile

4·The Liston Fights

THE FIRST FIGHT
FEBRUARY 1964

No story on these two fights can begin without the reader understanding the character and ominous personality of Charles (Sonny) Liston, then reigning Heavyweight Champion of the World, so let us address ourselves to understanding this glowering behemoth.

Charles (Sonny) Liston started out his life as a tough guy. A man who made his living by beating people to a senseless pulp. He was as mean and tough a man as has been produced by any northern ghetto. His start in life led him predictably to the penitentiary where, again, he dominated the scene with his fists. His reputation was intimidating even to the guards, and they circulated rumors about how he could take punishment and how he could inflict mortal wounds with his hands. It is not surprising, then, that he came to the attention of the Boys, who worked their wondrous ways and managed to obtain a parole for him and place him in the loving hands of one Frank (Blinky) Palermo of Philadelphia. Blinky, one of the *boys* in charge of the fistic division of their corporation, fed Sonny for a few lean years and taught him all he knew of the boxing scene, got him some competent cornermen and a few front-runners as managers, and leaned on a few promoters to use him. Presto, Sonny did the rest. In spite of, or perhaps because of, his background, the press took to Sonny as a welcome relief from the neurotic festivals of Floyd Patterson and his multiple emotional problems. Sonny was a man you could love and hate at the same time. He had a pure, uncomplicated yearning for mayhem. An identifiable, easy-to-write-about character who swept through the heavyweight division like the Wehrmacht through the Low Countries. Finally, even Floyd had to acknowledge his presence, and his finely honed predilection for self-destruction drove him to a confrontation with Sonny Liston. It also drove his cautious manager (who had carefully guided his cotton-candy career through the mediocre and amateurish opponents to a fairly long run as the heavyweight champ while ducking all real contenders and *especially* Charles [Sonny] Liston) into a premature retirement.

The first and second championship bouts were ghastly encounters whose principal features were the spectacle of the courageous but driven Floyd actively seeking the huge glove of Liston, and Liston obliging with predictable and depressingly similar results: Floyd down and out twice. Floyd, a student of nature, had apparently studied the Moth and the Flame. Whatever the reason, those two fights finished Floyd and made Sonny. Charles (Sonny) Liston emerged the most convincing heavyweight champion since Joe Louis, and I include Rocky Marciano, who was not so highly considered in the sports pages of his day. It wasn't until after his career was over that he was acclaimed as he is now. But Sonny was acclaimed then and there. He was tough, he was mean, he was unbeatable, he was champion of the world, and the underworld cheered *their boy*.

Sonny began to tour the world and make everyone a believer in his meanness; he took frank pleasure in inflicting personal harm on anyone who stood in his way. One story is typical of the Liston of that era, and I relate it to demonstrate the impression he left wherever he went.

Reggie Gutteridge, possibly the most knowledgeable English boxing writer and TV commentator, was in Liston's rooms at a posh London hotel when the conversation (if anyone really ever had a conversation with Liston while he was champion) turned to toughness. Reggie said he was pretty tough and Liston looked at him menacingly.

Now at the time Reggie was in his middle thirties. He was a small, kindly-looking man and in no way did he appear a threatening force, but Reggie had been a tough tanker in the war. He had lost part of a leg in action and wore a cork leg, although no one could ever guess that he had lost a leg unless he mentioned it.

Liston was still contemplating the small Englishman malevolently when, quite unexpectedly, Reggie picked up an icepick and drove it into his leg through the trouser leg.

Sonny reacted as expected and exclaimed, *"Hey! Man! Did you see what that mother-f——— did? Do that again, man!"*

Reggie calmly did it again and suggested that Sonny do the same to himself if he was as tough as they (he) said.

Sonny blinked as he contemplated the pain of an icepick through his huge calf muscles and slowly stood up. "Naw, man, I can't do that . . . but *you* can't do *this*."

And with that he wheeled and struck the huge oak door a resounding smash with his closed fists. The door, Reggie says, simply split in two and fell apart, and brought forth a hotel manager in a cutaway and striped pants with a receipt to sign immediately.

This was the Sonny Liston that a fresh-faced, innocent child-man named Cassius Clay decided to beard in his den. At first Liston was amused by his stunts and tricks, but when Clay actually went to Liston's home in Denver and woke up the Bear in his lair, that was too much even for Sonny, and he took the bait. Clay was the number one contender. He had earned the title shot; it was no gift. But Sonny had always thought Clay would have to grow up first before his people would let him get demolished by Sonny's awesome power. After all, the Kid did not possess a punch, and no one knew whether he had any toughness in him. He was not off the streets and was not, in any observable manner, a tough, aggressive kid. In fact, Clay was upset when his opponents would challenge him outside the ring, for he looked on boxing as a match, and not as a fight. He operated with surgical calm, and he had the equipment and the talent to do so. He could afford to divorce emotion from performance. He was never angry with his opponents; it was all a big game which he invariably won. The rage would come later with religious conviction. I am invariably astounded that religion, which professes kindness, always seems to evoke homicidal urges in men when they embrace the principles totally. But that is another story.

The Nilon brothers, frankfurter magnates from Philadelphia, had bought Liston's contract and now were managing Sonny in the absence of Blinky who was *away,* vacationing at government expense. They seized the opportunity to fight Cassius Clay with alacrity. The fight was to be held in Miami Beach at the height of the season, and both Liston and the Nilons felt they deserved a nice vacation while, on the side, disposing of this pesky intruder. The stage was set for the slapstick scenario that was to be a prime feature of all of Clay's fights thereafter.

Down in South Beach, the ghetto of the Jewish retired and poor, there exists a gym right out of a bad fight movie. It is upstairs over a drugstore and before you get to it, you can hear it and smell it. The Fifth Street Gym belongs to Angelo Dundee, and it has produced many top-flight fighters and more than its share of champions. The floors are raw wood, the paint rubbed off by countless rope-skipping feet, the walls in need of paint, the windows dirty with peeling, painted signs of boxing gloves, and the smell—there is the unmistakable smell of human perspiration mingled with rubbing alcohol. All in all, it is enough to make any dyed-in-the-wool boxing fan swoon with delight.

Cassius Clay brought his road show into town and into the Fifth Street Gym, and the place has never been the same. Cassius Clay drew a full house every day he trained. The writers began to appear and they were never short of material for the columns. *Playboy* sent down Leroy Neiman and Leroy, with his real feeling for fighters, recorded the scene with more clarity than the scribes with their words. Leroy stayed with the scene for six weeks and set a record that still holds for the Clay camp: he survived the entire period without once having to pick up a tab. That is what is known as living off one's talents—a much admired trait around boxing people, always chronically short of what is known in the financial world as *the ready*.

At the other end of the beach, Surfside, along with the well-established, well-heeled beachites, the Heavyweight Champion of the World, Charles (Sonny) Liston, was ensconced in luxury. In another era the presence of this glowering, ominous man would have sent half the beachites scurrying to their phones to call the cops, but now he was society's darling. His workouts were slovenly and consisted of his trainer, Willie Reddish, throwing a medicine ball with the force of a freight train against Liston's rippling abdomen. It did not occur to anyone that Clay had not thrown a body punch since the Olympics but, then again, you cannot toughen the eyebrows by throwing medicine balls at them, and this area was Clay's target. Liston would then skip rope to the leaden beat of "Night Train," a heavy Coleman Hawkins record of the time.

At the termination of this, Liston would pull up a chair to address the press and the audience, usually prefacing his remarks with "I don't know what I'm training so hard for; it ain't gonna last but a round."

Everyone would laugh and shout things like "Tear that loudmouth's head off, Sonny," and Sonny would wink and aim his finger like a cocked pistol. Then, in an uncharacteristic concession to the Nilon brothers' scheme for milking the title dry, the management would make Sonny pose with children for a buck or two a photo. I still have a picture of Sonny holding my son Ferdie, when he was not quite 2 years old, an enormous black hand holding this small white bundle like a farmer holding a wisp of cotton.

All manner of celebrities came to our camp to see what Clay was doing, but the highlight was the visit of a little-known group out of Liverpool. The Beatles came in late but, trailed by a huge retinue of followers, tore up the gym. I was struck by their pathetically skinny, sunburned bodies. They were very obliging and posed for all types of corny photos, and Clay, ever the showman, thought up gag photos that made all the papers. The birth of the Ali Circus occurred during these hectic weeks of preparation for the big, ugly Bear.

The Ali Circus starts six weeks before a fight. The hardiest of the takers begin to show up at camp. This one wants to be a cook, that one a bodyguard, that one a janitor, that one to take care of the equipment, this one to drive, this one to get "foxes," this one to spy, this one to photograph, and so it goes. Old fighters, old trainers, fans, idolators, job seekers. They come in wondrous profusion, and Clay lets them all stay. There is no control. No one can tell this kid anything. His heart is big, and his hand fast on the draw. Always got a buck for the brothers. Soon the training begins; by some strange process the real ones work their way through the phonies, and eventually the camp gets tight. We have the same cast with a few new taxi-squad additions, but the workers are in action. Then the press corps descends. Basically, they are all the same people for every fight. Once in a while there will be a new guy, totally out of his depth, sent by some magazine to get a "fresh" slant on Clay. Tell me what he is really like in two thousand words. Please. TV people swarm in as the fight nears, followed by the caravan of the stars— celebrities, politicians, well-known people. And, last, the people from the street who finally made it: the *action people*. Gamblers, pimps, hookers, connections, procurers, thieves, and the rest of their entourages. Now we are complete and ready to "go to war."

At this time and all through it, Ali was living in a small house in the northwest section of town. He loved to sit on the stoop of the porch and watch children come by and stare at him until he would lovingly scoop them up and talk to them. Every afternoon and morning it was like watching a kiddie show, and it was hard to tell who was benefiting the most. His house was the barracks for his camp. He housed the sparring partners among whom was a middleweight named Jimmy Ellis, who later grew into a heavyweight and took over Ali's title when he was forced to vacate it. Bundini and Solomon McAteer were then the trainers assisting Angelo Dundee, and they also lived in the house. At about this time a change came over Clay, and it affected the whole camp and the whole promotion.

Cassius Clay had been quietly observing the ghetto scene and the Fame and Fortune Syndrome for Blacks. He correctly saw that many brothers went straight to hell as soon as they became famous. Girls in battalion strength were thrown at them. They began to drink, or use drugs, and soon they vanished from the scene, discarded like an empty milk carton. What could he do differently? His religion, the Baptist religion of his folks, did not seem to be a solution, perpetuating, as it did, a white-based philosophy with no equal status room for blacks. No, religion was worse—a greased slide downhill. Clay was basically an innocent man, openhearted and childlike in his naïve approach to life, too ready to believe anything told him by a brother, and too suspicious of whites, who were always suspect in his eyes. Where could he find something to believe in that fitted his needs as a pure athlete and made him comfortable? It was a problem about to be solved.

Cassius Clay has a brother, Rudolph Valentino Clay, and he loves him dearly and guides him in all things of this world, but in this instance his brother led Cassius into the light. Hanging around Red's Barber Shop on the Avenue, Rudy had run across the hustling messenger of the faith in the form of Captain Sam. Now Captain Sam, who worked part time at Hialeah, shining shoes, had his Theology straight and when he gave the message of the Black Muslim faith to Rudy, the latter hung on every word and took the message home to Cassius Clay, who perked up his ears and wanted to hear more. Rapidly, Cassius Clay saw the reason and the beautiful fulfillment of his dream. Here he had a religion that was good for the athlete and great for the black man. Eagerly he joined, and painlessly Cassius Clay died and the metamorphosis to Muhammad Ali was complete in less time than it takes to write about it.

Here I must pause again to explain in simplistic fashion what the Black Muslims were all about, and what effect they were to have on Ali and the Liston fights.

The Black Muslims were born in a penitentiary when a frail, slim black man named Elijah Muhammad, serving a brief sentence for draft evasion, had time to contemplate the teachings of another black man who thought he was God or God's Messenger on earth. This frail, asthmatic man saw all too well the message when the originator vanished, and he assumed the leadership of the then unknown Black Muslims. It was after the War, and he correctly foresaw that the black man in America must have strong leadership, and that this leadership must preach superiority of the black race, and that the main underlying theme must be the "Black Is Beautiful" one. If racist slogans were needed, he provided them. If the white men must become White Devils in order to enlist the strong, then so be it. And if the religion needed some myths to believe in, then he created some, such as the *Mother Ship* idea which, on the surface, seems inspired by the then popular Flash Gordon strip. I find that people laugh at this until I point out that our religions are rife with this sort of improbable myth. If you can believe in Jonah in the whale and Noah in the Ark, the burning bushes, and fifty thousand tuna fish sandwiches and twenty thousand Dr. Peppers from a sliver of bread and water, then I propose that the Mother Ship is not too unusual to believe in. Ali certainly believes it and will point it out to you on clear nights.

He did it on a cold night in Finland once, fighting an exhibition outdoors in a valley. Ali stopped the fight to clinch with his sparring partner, Jimmy Ellis, and nod to a pinpoint of light seemingly suspended from on high. "The Mother Ship, Jimmy; it's watching over us," and he pointed with a gloved hand to the beacon of light. At that, the whole rim of the arena lit up with multiple lights. The ring being down in the valley and the arena surrounded, as it was, by tall trees, kids without the prices of admission had scaled the trees and were watching their hero way down below. One had tested his powerful light and, when it caught Ali's eye, he had pointed, whereupon all the other kids did the same and lit their flashlights and matches. On the whole, it wasn't a good night for the Mother Ship theory.

Anyhow, whatever the means to enable the black man to overcome his inferiority complex and to quit emulating the white man, Elijah Muhammad adopted it. If some of the means were harsh, the ends seemed to justify them. It was not a society of weak-kneed sob sisters. It was a society of street fighters, of toughs and, yes, at the beginning, of con men who thought they were in on the ground floor of yet another religion to milk the ghetto dollar reserve. But it is perhaps an interesting thought that here is a religion that started as a con game and ended up straight, whereas the converse is often the case in our white society.

Elijah was helped by a series of brilliant black men who took these teachings seriously. The best was Malcolm X, and he set his sights on the greatest prize of all, Cassius Clay, soon to be Muhammad Ali. When Malcolm broke with Elijah and formed his own group, he tried to entice Ali to his camp. It has never been proven that the bullets he took soon afterward were related to the situation, but merely that these events occurred in that sequence.

You must also know that until Ali came into camp the Black Muslims were considered a fringe lunatic group close to the kamikazes and the Fuzzy-Wuzzies, even by their own black brothers in *Ebony*. They were, in a few words, *a tough bunch.*

The promoters of this fight were rubbing their hands in glee, anticipating a killing of, at the very least, a financial nature. The promoter on Miami Beach for years and years was the dynamo brother of Angelo Dundee, Chris Dundee, He had worked his winning ways on a millionaire sportsman, Bill McDonald, and he had come up with the money to back the fight, which was a natural from the start. Cassius Clay had a million dollars' worth of advance publicity. Half the country wanted him to win just to knock off this assassin villain who had terrorized all the heavyweights in the world. The other half would pay as much to see him get his cage cleaned. Nobody liked Sonny Liston, the Thug, so the match was a natural. Chris put it succinctly: the White Hat against the Black Hat. Of such things are million-dollar gates made.

Then, suddenly, a black cloud obscured the golden horizon

—or should I say a Black Muslim cloud? Frantic phone calls poured in to the Louisville group. Is Cassius Clay a Black Muslim? Is such a thing possible? Ask Angelo, he should know, and so all eyes turned to Angelo for a hint.

In fifteen years of working with Angelo, I have observed one thing: He is the most absorbed man in what he is doing in boxing. A lion can come in the gym, but if he is watching a perfect jab or an inadequate bob and weave, he will not notice. The Ali training was a sample of this. Angelo was so intent on getting his man ready for the Bear that he could not see the Wolf. It reached the ludicrous extreme of Angelo warning Ali that some guy was hanging around named Captain Sam who was supposed to be something bad called a Black Muslim, not knowing or suspecting that Ali was already a Muslim and Captain Sam his mentor.

Slowly the awful truth hit all the parties, and the promotion threatened to blow up if the kid did not renounce his faith and say publicly that he was not a Muslim. In the first of many such morally courageous steps, Ali staunchly refused to do this and the fight of his dreams, and his championship, and all he worked for, was called off. He went home to pack, his exterior not giving a hint of what was going on inside him. In a horrifying moment, the million-dollar dream had turned into a nightmare.

"Now we have a Black Hat against a Black Hat," moaned Chris Dundee, and as usual he was right. The public would cheerfully have plunked down the two hundred fifty dollars for a ringside seat if they could have witnessed a double knockout.

Reason and avarice prevailed at the last moment, and the fight was on again. Joy swept the little house in the northwest section and the house, now tightly packed with brothers in black suits and narrow ties, rejoiced and played endless tapes of Elijah Muhammad's messages. There is no record of the reaction at the Surfside camp of the Bear. Probably a bored yawn as the Bear prepared to dispatch the fresh kid with one well-aimed haymaker.

The weigh-in at a heavyweight champion fight is an empty ceremony devoid of meaning since there is no weight limit; it is just a means of getting the boys together to see how they measure up and to give the press a chance to write some stuff and hype up the promotion. That is the way it had been since time immemorial. Ali changed that. Henceforth all Ali weigh-ins ranged from high drama to low comedy, but they were never dull!

We gathered in the now bulging house and everyone was in a state of extreme excitement. The veterans of the campaigns were there. Ali's friends since the beginning, the talented photographer Howard Bingham was so nervous he wasn't stuttering. Lowell Riley, a grim useful adjunct to the camp, was Herbert Muhammad's man on the scene, and several of the original troop were on the fringes, intimidated by the Muslim bodyguards. They would soon be discarded and, in some cases, disappear altogether. Bundini was reaching a peak of frenzied excitement and his exhortations, always poetic in the past, took on the gibberish quality of a Zulu cheerleader about to launch himself on a British fort. Angelo was unaware of the change in the troop since he had his highly professional mind working on the practical details of the weigh-in and of the psychological warfare that was about to begin. Sugar Ray Robinson, a former hero of Ali's youth, brought in at heavy expense, was attempting to talk some sense of decorum into the young kid. Ali listened attentively, nodding his head vigorously in agreement. Yes, yes, this was the biggest event of his life and the biggest sports event of the year; yes sir, yes sir, he was aware that he had acted childishly in the past but this was for the whole bowl of wax, and no sir, he would not do anything to bring disgrace on his race or on Sugar Ray or any of the other pros who were with him. Yes, yes, and f——— off, Sugar Ray.

At the door of the Miami Beach Convention Hall, the same place he had, as a raw beginner pro, stepped in to work with Ingo Johansson as a sparring partner and beaten the hell out of him, he paused to take stock of the scene. Over eight hundred newsmen from all over the world were in attendance. TV cameras were focusing on the door when he hit it at full stride, Bundini struggling to keep up, hanging onto his robe belt like a baby to its umbilical cord, and both at full voice, shouting their war slogans, and for the millionth time: *Float like a butterfly, sting like a bee, rumble, young man, rumble! AuuuuGGuuuuuuuuuuu!*

Sonny's head snapped around and he was reduced to a mere spectator at his own weigh-in. The war of nerves had been won. Sonny was down for the count. His most feared psychological ploy was taken from him and he could no longer stand in a commanding perch, glaring menacingly down on a cowed adversary. Soon the place was in pandemonium. Most reporters had picked Sonny; in fact, only eight in all out of the eight hundred had picked Ali, and one brash newcomer to TV, Bob Halloran, picked him more out of youthful contrariness than from any process of logical thought.

Now they were literally nose to nose and, surprise of surprises, Ali was *taller* and *bigger* than the Bear. As has happened to many a hapless victim, Sonny underestimated Ali's size because of his baby features and his smooth, unmuscled body. Sonny used to put several towels under his robe to make him look bigger and more intimidating, as if that were necessary!

Now Ali was touching the Bear! Newsmen instinctively recoiled. There goes the fight, everyone thought, as Ali taunted, yelled at, and generally unnerved Liston, who could not believe what was happening to his act. Bundini excelled in this moment for he had a never-ending variety of catchy phrases and a loud mouth, and although he was safely behind Ali, he was not cowed or scared by Liston and made it obvious to all. Sugar Ray fought to keep from falling off the stage, not the first to be knocked off a stage by the runaway team of Ali and Bundini. Angelo smiled helplessly at the press. He knew the act was killing Liston, and he loved it. To his credit, he has never stopped a winning ploy and is willing to do anything to win his fight. Angelo Dundee was one of the few fight people there who *knew* Ali was going to win. Many thought he might, but none knew it, and certainly none admitted thinking it before the fight. *After* the fight, the experts who picked Ali were plentiful.

At this point in the story, it is well to reflect on how good newspapermen become pundits. They simply predict a fact and then work like hell to make their prediction come true. Consider the case of the late Jimmy Cannon. Jimmy was one helluva writer but not the most lovable of men, and acid is the word that springs to mind when I think of little Jimmy Cannon embattled on all fronts, mad at the airlines that brought him, the hotel that housed him, the restaurant that fed him, the promotion, the promoters, the fighters, his colleagues, and generally mad at the world. Get the picture? Jimmy was tough to get along with but, boy, could he write! And, better, he could make a story happen.

In this instance, Jimmy had been writing that Ali was scared to death and, ergo, his act was one of a hysterical man on the way to the gallows. Many bought this and also wrote this, and so a spark was born. At the time of the weigh-in, the doctor on the Miami Beach Boxing Commission was Dr. Alex Robbins, an irascible man with a no-nonsense approach. His family were all doctors and that does something to a man right there. Dr. R was known to wager a fiver on a fight from time to time but no one had the temerity to suggest that this could affect the outcome of a fight if one of the men were cut, and on the whole he was a competent fight doctor. Imagine his chagrin when he had to examine Ali and found his blood pressure to be 200/100 and his pulse galloping out of control. The fight was again threatened. What was the cause of these unseemly numbers? Dr. Robbins was stuck, and while he surreptitiously looked under the table at his Merck manual under "Hypertension, Heavyweights," Jimmy Cannon slid in the chair next to his and whispered, "Could it be that the kid is scared to death, Doc?"

A small bulb lit in Dr. Robbins' head and he nodded gravely. "Yes, yes, Mr. Cannon, this fighter is scared to death and if his blood pressure is the same at fight time, it is all off."

Pandemonium. Canceled again. Chris and McDonald retreat to their office and worry about overdosing on two-hundred-fifty-dollar tickets; the Louisville group runs en masse to Angelo and appoints me to go to the house with Ali and take blood pressure hourly to assure everyone that he is OK in case of litigation.

The ride back to the house is pure joy. Bundini and the crowd are in high spirits. They are sure they whipped the ole Bear's head good. Ali is in great spirits. We enter into the house. Clots of conservatively dressed men are lounging around, listening to the exhortations of the Messenger to kill the White Devils. I walk through this into Ali's bedroom and cannot help feeling like a Jew delivering laundry to Dachau. Ali smiles serenely and thrusts out his massive arm. I take my first blood pressure: 120/80. Normal.

I look at Ali, cool as a snake (are they cool or do they just look it?) and smiling. I try to look serious. "Why did you do that, Ali? Why did you act so nutty up there in front of all those people?"

He leans forward, whispering, in the time-honored way that both gets your attention and commands your respect.

"Because Liston thinks I am a *nut*. He is scared of no man, but he is scared of a *nut* because he doesn't know what I am going to do."

It is well to insert a personal note here so that you can reflect on the odd circumstances that affect the world of high finance. Seldom does it come to the occasional bettor to "get well" on a sure thing. First, there are no sure things, and when they are close to sure things, you have to lay a big price to get on, or, to the uninformed, one must wager a sum of money that is large to win a sum that is small, and if you lose, you lose a lot. Seldom does it work the other way around, and you get to risk a small sum but gain a large sum in return if you win. The last sure bet like that was when the U.S.A. was a 3–1 underdog to lose World War II a few minutes after Pearl Harbor, but by morning the prices had gone back to 5–6 pick 'em because some heavy money had come in on the U.S.A. from Moscow Joe. But that is another story.

Ali was a 6–1 underdog. Basically, this means that if you bet one hundred dollars on Ali and he won, you would win six hundred. Although I was no novice to boxing betting, having lost a quarter to my maid on Max Baer over Joe Louis, I was not as active now due to my growing involvement in boxing, and I would not bet on a fight I had to work in for fear it would impair my judgment. I have since found out that this is pure bullshit since most people who work fights bet on them out of some sense of loyalty to their fighter. This does not cover certain cornermen who bet on the other guy. I have no saving answer for them. In any case, I had made up my mind to bet a sizable chunk on Ali because of a firm opinion that was forming in my mind that Liston did not stand a chance against this wacky kid. The day I am at present outlining had almost run its course, and I was still locked in with Ali; Bundini and Solomon also wanted to bet and each gave me a C-note to put down at 6 to 1. I had not yet done that since I was waiting for a better price. I am the eternal optimist. Six to one! My god, I had to wait ten years before another sucker bet like that came my way, and then I was in Africa and couldn't get down.

About the time I was going to call a surcease to my vigil and go home to bathe and get ready, an emergency came up. Some stewardess called to say she was pregnant and was going to tell all to the press. There was a momentary panic since there were no cars outside to transport the troops to reason with the poor, timid, frightened child and convince her she must be mistaken. The mistake was twofold: Ali was not the father and she had no chance to pull off her game. It didn't take long to spy my new car, a Lincoln Continental Town model that looked like it was made for Frank Costello. The boys asked for and got the keys. Off they went and I didn't see my car for two days. From the look of it when I got it back, I assumed the boys had driven to Havana for a quick A/B. At any rate, the obstetrical problem was handled somehow by someone else, and meanwhile we saddled up and rode to the auditorium, where things were Grimsville.

Ali stood in the back of the auditorium, looking on as his kid brother took a fearful shellacking in a preliminary. Ali muttered to himself, "He'll never fight again. I'll take care of him. Never again. No more fights."

Actually Rudy did fight again, but against his brother's strongest objections.

Soon we were locked into the dressing room and the scene was scary, but I didn't learn why until later. The room was sealed. No one could come in or out. In the room were Ali, Rahaman (Rudy), Bundini, Sarria (the silent, efficient Cuban masseur), Angelo, and myself. Occasionally a familiar face would be allowed to pop in, but it was a solemn time, and now the ritual of the water bottle began.

Ali had assigned Rahaman to watch the heavily taped

water bottle but at times, distracted as he was, Rahaman would take his eyes off the bottle and Ali would order him to untape it and refill it. Again and again this process was repeated. Finally, he reached a point where both brothers had to go into a Muslim prayer and, of course, in these small confines it was difficult to find room so Ali slipped into a shower stall. Another dilemma. Which way was east? I said I thought the hot water was east and the cold water west and that seemed to satisfy everyone, thereby setting new indoor criteria for direction finding in a dressing room.

Many years later I asked Ali why the water bottle act, and he gave me a curious answer that seemed to make sense. All that day he had been receiving phone calls from the brothers up north saying his White Enemies were going to get him; they had worked themselves up to a high pitch of paranoia. Now, confronted by two white men in his dressing room, he has to pause and consider the possibility of a sellout by the White Devils—in this case, Angelo and me. When I pointed out we could have both doped him in many ways before the fight, he in turn pointed out that even brothers turn against brothers for money, and no one was free from suspicion. Later in the evening this type of thinking almost got Angelo one king-sized beating, or worse, as we will presently see.

Time was up and we walked into the arena. There was tension in the air but of a different nature than that of a genuine championship fight between two equal men—for example, the Ali-Frazier fight. The tension was electric, but this tension was more like that of an audience at a hanging. They were here to see this kid get his. *When* he was going to get it was the only question. In the corner Ali was tense, as he had every right to be since he had placed himself way out on a limb. That turned out to be his custom in all major fights. It inspired him, apparently, to cut off all possibility of retreat. It was his night and he knew it but there was still the matter of executing his plan, and the Bear looked bigger and bigger and meaner and meaner. The time was drawing near and Bundini was off to the side, glowering at the Bear, putting his own brand of voodoo on the Bear. Said Bear looked over and gave him a lethal look like saying, "And after him, *you* are next, chump." Angelo was busy gloving up his man and I watched Sonny glove up. Solomon and Sarria were busy fussing around the corner, and suddenly they were in the middle of the ring. The bell rang before I was ready for it and my heart humped up in my throat. Could he *really* do it?

The first round passed like a blur. The blur was Ali dancing, kicking out a stinging jab, occasionally a solid right. The Bear went all out. Hadn't he said he would get this kid in *one?* Rumor had it Liston had a big wager on himself to knock out this kid in one. Well, if he did, he went back to his corner immeasurably poorer, for at the end of round one Liston was puffing and Ali was coasting along like a road runner on fresh batteries. Rounds two and three were more of the same except that Liston seemed resigned to a longer night and went back to the basic body attack. After the fight, Sarria would be called to the little house to massage a sore Ali, his flanks and ribs one big, angry red welt. The Bear could certainly hit. But even then Ali could take body shots and keep dancing. He was a human tank on ballet dancer legs. Then a strange thing happened and Angelo went from goat to hero in a few seconds.

Liston had apparently injured his shoulder and they were putting alcohol and oil of wintergreen on it. Ali got some on his brow. As Angelo performed the cornerman's ritual of wiping his man's face with a sponge, he got a drop in his eye. This burns like pure fire and soon both eyes were red and blurring fast. Ali turned to Bundini, sure that the White

Establishment had gotten to him, and said, "Cut them off," meaning his gloves. Bundini, stupefied by the horrific turn of events, looked uncomprehending.

The referee came over and yelled above the din, "If you don't get up in ten seconds, you lose this fight on a TKO."

Now Angelo, halfway down the ring stairs, with one hand on Ali's butt pushed him up, with the other took his stool, and Ali stood blinking, blind, and at the mercy of the murderous Bear. The crowd roared and I swore most of that roar came from Liston, who looked at Ali like a kid looks at a new bike on Christmas. Ali stumbled forth, groping for Liston. Liston swung a haymaker which Ali instinctively ducked, and so the round went, Ali reeling, Liston coming on, but by the end of the round a strange thing happened. Ali's eyes began to clear and Liston began to get tired; finally, the kid was popping hard lefts to Liston's face which began to puff and cut below the eye, and suddenly he looked his age. Liston said he was approaching 35, but he didn't say from which direction.

In the meantime we were having our own drama in the corner; I overheard two tough-looking Fruits of Islam plan a nasty surprise for Angelo for having cost them the fight. They contended that Angelo had something in the sponge. I shouted to Angelo to rub his eyes to show them it wasn't in the sponge. He didn't hear me and the threats were now getting serious. Finally, Angelo's brother Jimmy heard me and motioned to Angelo, who then performed the sponge-in-the-eye routine for them, which quieted them down but did not fully convince them. Fortunately we won, thereby sparing them the agony of trying to decide whether to kill him or merely maim him.

The next two rounds were all ours and Liston, seeing the handwriting on the wall, did what all bullies are programmed to do when the going gets tough: *He quit.* Now one might say that Ali tried to quit. I think you can see that this does not apply here. Ali was young and blinded, facing a man who had a reputation as a killer, and whom he had goaded into a murderous, homicidal state. Liston quit with all his faculties intact. He quit to fight another day. And so it was that he robbed Ali of credibility. No one believed he had done this impossible thing. We now had to do it again.

As a final note to this glorious night, let me remind the reader of those preceding paragraphs on high finance and opportunities lost. You will note that I was locked in with Ali since early afternoon and never had a chance to place my bet, or those of Bundini and Solomon, and so it came to pass that the fight cost me (one of the Believers) twelve hundred dollars since I was not about to tell Bundini and Solomon that I had not placed their bets, and one hundred dollars at 6 to 1, and so on. As you young fans can see, it is not financially sound to bet on prizefights. Strange things happen; you may end up locked in a dressing room with a contender and not be able to place the bet.

THE SECOND LISTON FIGHT
MAY 1965

The first Liston fight made Muhammad Ali the Heavyweight Champion of the World but he did not receive the recognition he felt that achievement merited. This was because Liston had quit and the ever cynical sports public accepted it as proof of still another fight game fix. To this point Ali's whole career was suspect to the man on the street. The idea of picking rounds smelled of fix and a cheap con game like the wrestling racket. Now the brash young braggart had laid low the mighty, unbeatable, murderous Sonny Liston. No, that was too much to accept. The sportswriters, 90 percent wrong in their evaluation of Ali, uncomfortable with his new racist

69

religion, took to feeding this disbelief with sly digs and in-nuendos, and the signing of a rematch added fuel to the fire since it now appeared obvious why Liston quit. He was look-ing forward to another payday.

The first problem was where to find a bombproof place to hold the fight. In the early sixties the violence which was to sweep that decade was just getting warmed up, and every racist worth his salt, and a few religious zealots and self-styled patriots, felt it their duty to take a shot at this kid for what he dared to flaunt in the face of America. Bomb threats came and went and Ali, setting a pattern that was to see him through all of his multiple problems, blithely decided to ignore things he had no control over and get to the thing he could control: his boxing career.

Ali trained for the second fight in Miami Beach. The Ali Circus had grown amazingly in the few months since he won the championship. Ali seemed to enjoy it and exulted in his newly won fame. He was a big name now and loved every minute but he had not lost the common touch, as he never would, and still loved to mingle with working stiffs and chil-dren and to "shock and amaze" people by going out of his way to be nice to them—for the pure joy of watching their faces light up with recognition.

"Say, ain't you Cassius Clay?"

Ali would smile his million-dollar smile and say, "No, I am *Muhammad Ali . . . champion of the whole wide world.*"

The first round of the second Liston fight was won by Ali inadvertently when he suffered a hernia days before the fight, which had to be postponed for three months. Now Liston may have been a little long in the tooth but he had reached the peak condition of his career. He was lean, mean, and ready. He could not maintain such a condition for another two or three months and he knew it. Try as he might, he would never be as sharp and strong again. Strangely enough, as we shall see, the same thing in reverse happened to Ali as he sought to reclaim *his* title from Foreman in Africa. Ali was old but at his peak, yet when Foreman cut his eye and the fight had to be postponed for another month, Ali did not fall apart. But this is a story that comes later.

The site was finally chosen. The *fight* was to be inflicted on Lewiston, Maine. The town was small and inadequate but no one wanted this fight with all its menacing overtones in *their* city, so the hapless citizens of Lewiston went to the mattress. The town filled up on fight day—more lawmen and press than fight fans. It was a dismal failure at the box office. The Garden would have sold out but the fight was too controversial, and it transcended a mere fight. People were not used to controversy in their champions. The days of the simple, uncomplicated, good and true champions like Louis and Marciano were just past, and the people had not as yet accepted the individuality of a man like Ali.

A small crowd gathered and sat through "The Star-Spangled Banner." Ali returned to his corner and turning to the east offered his Muslim prayer, with gloves upturned.

The fight began with a trim, fleet Ali circling, and a ponderous Liston chasing him in a circle with his familiar Chicago-style shuffle. His timing was predictable in that he had to shuffle forth with two steps, and on the third throw a left jab. Set and repeat. Ali was there through the first two steps but was gone by the third, and Liston was whistling that heavy artillery jab into the still Lewiston air. Two and a half minutes into the round, Liston had caught a few good Ali counterpunches but had not landed anything effective and was becoming impatient and abandoned in his attack. At this moment the Phantom Punch was uncorked.

Ali had a cute maneuver wherein he used the rope to play off of and simultaneously threw a sneaky short overhand right over an opponent's extended left jab. I have seen him do this in the gym hundreds of times, catching fighters completely off guard and stung with this cutie move, but I must confess I never saw anybody go down with that shot. Now, many years later, looking at the films for the hundredth time, I see Liston's face turn with the punch, his eyes blink, and then he loses his equilibrium and falls. At the time I did not see anything but Liston falling. I understood what the initial rhubarb was about but, friends, Liston *was* hit that one-in-a-million shot. Even Liston was mortal and even he had one spot that would short-circuit his brain for an instant. I know the arguments, and I think they are all based on sound human reasoning and logic, but in a heavyweight championship fight throw all that out the window. Yes, I agree, Ali is not a devastating puncher but when he has to, when the real chips are down, when it's do-or-die, Ali knocks them *out*. Not the lesser lights that come to tilt with the windmill, but the real threats, and in this manner he stopped the unstoppable and the unknockoutable: *Liston, Foreman,* and *Frazier*. Defense rests.

Back to the pandemonium. Liston rests on his back, momentarily looking up into another world. The referee moves in to start his count, but wait, several factors which have been overlooked now come to light and have a terrific impact on this travesty. First, the referee is Jersey Joe Walcott, the old champ, in for a fast payday. Nice as a celebrity; wrong as a referee. He had never handled a fight of this magnitude. Referees are true professionals, and there is no such thing as a good amateur, celebrity referee. They should all be banned in important fights. Because a man has had many fights does not make him a referee any more than a man who has been through many operations on his body is a surgeon. The referee literally controls two fighters' lives. Incompetence, a slight hesitation, can cause a ring death or permanent injury. No, Walcott should not have been there. The best referee in the world has a hard time controlling Ali even now, but in those wild-eyed days it took a super referee to control the fight. And so it happened that Walcott let this fight slip out from under him.

When Liston fell, Ali was supposed to go to a neutral corner. Until he did so, no count could begin. Dempsey-Tunney Long Count Fight: Chapter and Verse. Ali was as skeptical as his public, and he stood over Liston in disbelief. He waved him up with his gloved hand, and snarled at him repeatedly:

"Get up, you bum! No one will believe this!"

Walcott made some desperate efforts to wave the wild-eyed Ali to a neutral corner, while trying to keep a count going. He looked with desperation at the timekeeper, whose job it was to count the seconds by the clock. Again, a fatal flaw in the procedure.

The timekeeper was an aged citizen whose last effort at timekeeping might well have been keeping time at a three-day boat race in Bangor, and he was as flustered as Walcott.

Liston rolled over like a decerebrate beached whale, and did not get up, keeping his eyes on Ali all the while. Ali, unflinching, was glowering over the fallen Liston. Sonny was looking sheepishly up at him but not getting up. Walcott was doing a comic head-wagging bit, looking to the timekeeper, to Ali, to Liston, and back. Nothing much was being resolved, and Liston looked like he was down for the month, when out of the press section came the voice of authority to solve the dilemma.

A small thin man, aged but clear of voice, strode forward (the part to be played by Sam Jaffe in the movie version) and announced to Walcott, "The fight is over! Liston is out! *Ali wins!"*

The pressman was the redoubtable Nat Fleischer of *Ring* magazine, the historian and beloved Old Man of boxing journalism. I respectfully submit that he was in somewhat less than an authoritative position, and had absolutely no official say-so in this matter, but both the timekeeper and Walcott were so relieved to see an end to their problem that they gratefully concurred.

In the meantime, seventeen seconds had elapsed since Liston's thundering fall, and even Ali had backed off a moment. Liston, tired of his recumbent position, rested and, considering the matter of his payday, got up and started to fight again. Ali obliged while Walcott was over trying to hear what Nat was talking about. Walcott understands and goes over to stop the fight: "The *winner* and still *Heavyweight Champion of the World, Muhammad Ali!*" Pandemonium again.

On the sound track of this movie one hears a winded and exuberant Ali narrate a replay of the first round, but the film is wound back too far and he has to say inconsequential things while his image runs about the ring and then, suddenly, the phantom punch and Liston is down again, and Ali, looking and narrating the film minutes after the actual happening, misses the punch, as we all did, but recovers and says to the listening world, "I'm so fast, I missed the punch myself."

To recap what happened, and in the following epilogue an explanation from the man himself. Liston, desperate to put a good one on Ali, overextended his long jab. Ali, bouncing off the ropes, threw a short right over the jab which momentarily and very positively stunned Liston and he fell down, but not out. Ali stood over him. Walcott could not control Ali. Stop there. The count should not have continued until Ali went to a neutral corner. *He never did go to a neutral corner.* The fight was stopped by a nonofficial. No pressman had ever stopped a fight before, or since. The fight should have continued. Liston could have gotten up but didn't. Why? We shall soon see.

EPILOGUE

It is a few years later in Oakland, California. Ali has been stripped of his title because of his draft stand. His former sparring partner, Jimmy Ellis, is fighting Jerry Quarry for the vacated title in the finals of an elimination tournament. Coincidental with this event, Sonny Liston has petitioned the California Boxing Commission to reinstate his license, and the hearing takes place in the commission offices. No script-writer could duplicate that farce, and understanding the comic potential of that charade, I persuade Howard Cosell to go with me to the hearing.

Sonny walks in accompanied by a black Chicago attorney. Sonny is well dressed in his neat and surprisingly conservative manner. The lawyer is slick and one cannot help but notice that his skin is the same color as his briefcase. He opens the case, extracts a rather lengthy document, and begins to address the assembly like Clarence Darrow in a first-degree murder trial. There are a lot of wherefores flying and the general picture of Sonny Liston being drawn by the attorney compares favorably with Mother Cabrini, and the image of Liston is beginning to glow like a phosphorescent saint statue when Sonny growls in his dinosaur fashion, "Cut the bullshit; let 'em ask what they want."

The attorney looks at Sonny as if he is seeing him for the first time, but their eyes meet and he gets Sonny's meaning loud and clear. He shuts up.

A commissioner starts with the first question:

"Mr. Liston, do you know a Frank Palermo?"

"No."

"What?"

"I said no."

"Mr. Liston, you do not know Mr. Palermo of Philadelphia, Pennsylvania?"

"No."

"Mr. Liston, you have never talked to Mr. Frank Palermo?"

"No."

"Mr. Liston, you never had any business dealings with Mr. Frank Palermo, never talked to him, never asked his advice, never socialized with him?"

"No."

"Mr. Liston, you never ate in his place for three years following your parole from jail? He never kept you? Fed you? Trained you, taught you boxing? You don't remember Frank Palermo?"

"*Oh . . . you mean Blinky. . . . Oh, sure, Blinky was my man.*"

Established an underworld connection of the worst kind. Case dismissed. But, no, California was intent on giving Sonny back his license. This was in the days before Reagan.

Again the same commissioner: "Mr. Liston, have you ever heard the word *fix* used in connection with a fight?"

"No."

"Have you heard the words *tank job?*"

"No."

"*In the water?*"

"No."

"*Take a dive?*" (By now the commissioner's voice is starting to crack.)

"Oh . . . *you mean the Lewiston fight. . . . Yeah, I can tell you what happened there. . . .* Ali knocked me down with a sharp punch. . . . I was down but not hurt . . . but I looked up and saw Ali standing over me . . . now there is no way to get up from the canvas that you are not exposed to a great shot. Ali is waiting to hit me, the ref can't control him . . . I have to put one knee and one glove on the canvas to get up."

At this point he gets out of his chair and demonstrates. The public leans forth, the commissioners all lean forth to see this, and all are nodding in agreement with what Sonny is saying, and we can see that all the sympathy in that room is with Sonny and his plight, there on the floor, his chance of recovering his title slipping by as an incompetent ref wrestles with Attila the Hun. And now Liston gets to the punch line. It is as if he has been dreaming about this for years and has defined what happened to him in one sentence that clarifies and exculpates him from all human responsibility for that awful, shameful, emasculating moment in his life when he went from Liston the Terrible to Liston the Dog. Eyes narrowed, he leans forward, and in a confidential semiwhisper:

"You know Ali is a *nut*. . . . You can tell what a normal man is going to do, *but you can't tell what a nut is going to do* . . . and Ali is a *nut!*"

Liston leans back triumphantly as the gathered crowd suppresses the urge to break out in applause, and Liston nods his head in one last great affirmation of this truth that explains away the unexplainable.

The commissioner gavels the board to order. Put it to a vote. *Aye, Aye, Aye, Aye.* And from the back of the room, in the men's room, a muffled "Aye." Unanimous. Sonny Liston reinstated.

Sonny went on to a tragic end in Las Vegas, which was truly sad because in the end you had to like old Sonny, with his surly, menacing look, and his sweet, intelligent wife by his side, guiding him, taming his wilder impulses, and making Sonny almost seem human. I hated to see him go out that way, but Las Vegas is bad news for more than ex-champs, and Sonny simply learned the lesson the hard way.

In case you missed it, let me point out the final fact. Ali won the battle of nerves by his unusual performance at the first weigh-in, when he correctly thought that he could intimidate Liston by acting the nut, and in the end he got him twice. As we shall see, it is part of Ali's indescribable luck to do things for one reason while the action turns out totally right for him in another area, and this certainly was one of the bigger ones.

Eleven years later I was at my home talking into my tape machine for Richard Durham, who was co-authoring a book with Ali on his spectacular life, and we got to this story I have just related. Ali is listening and I can see he is very happy with the story but a bit puzzled, so I ask him why he is puzzled and he says, "That was good, Doc, but I don't remember saying that to you after the weigh-in about Liston being scared by a *nut*."

5·The Exile Years, 1967–1970— The Marciano–Ali Computer Fight

No one but Ali knows where the idea was born to resist the draft for the Vietnam war, but once the decision was made it persisted. Ali refused to be inducted into the army in Houston, Texas, and so began the long exile.

One of my colleagues was assigned to give Ali the induction intelligence exam. Ali did extremely poorly, so poorly that it was decided he must have been faking, and he was asked to take it again. The results were the same. Typically, Ali explained, "I said I was the *greatest*—not the *smartest!*"

Ali had gone through a divorce and had been totally indoctrinated into the Muslim faith, but he had nevertheless remained basically his irrepressible self. Now his very identity was being taken away, and again he withstood this severe test of character, but almost surely the revocation of his boxing license hurt him worse than he imagined it would. Life was not much fun when he had been shorn of the titles that assured him of his importance, as boxer and world champion. Then, during the exile years, two events transpired that undoubtedly fueled his efforts to return to the ring and win back his title.

The first of these events was the Marciano-Ali computer fight, staged by Murray Woroner of Miami. The idea was sound and entertaining, and the man responsible was a clever old radio man who had produced some inventive radio tapes before. They had involved simulated hour-by-hour reporting of the birth of Christ, and other world-shaking events done in contemporary style.

There existed only two undefeated heavyweight champions in the history of the game, and by a stroke of luck they were both close enough to the same age bracket so that it was possible to film the two in a simulated fight. The computer would be fed information by a panel of hand-picked boxing experts who had seen both fighters fight in their prime, and because of the relative youth of both fighters this did not prove an obstacle. The results would then be adapted to the screen by some clever script writing and the fighters would enact the scenes as written. It all seemed amazingly simple and a quick way to pick up a few easy bucks.

Murray Woroner is a quick-witted, energetic, imaginative man who has a way with a camera, and a fight freak of the first water, so that all of us felt that the results would be worth the work. Angelo was to be the only cornerman for Ali, Chris Dundee was to be the referee, and I was the ring doctor (unseen and unheard). The filming took a week or so, and the two principals were having the time of their lives. Rocky Marciano was by this time around forty, but he had the fierce pride of the tough champion that he was, and in preparation for this "fight" he actually went into training, losing the excess blubber that the years had put on, and even went to the extreme of buying a beautiful rug (hairpiece) which must have been tacked in because he never lost it no matter how hard they fought. On the other hand, Ali was still young and not as conscious of the spare tire around his middle, so that the results of looking at the stills from this effort are somewhat amazing in that Marciano looks like the young active fighter and Ali looks like the retired champion.

Initially the filming went beautifully, and both the fighters were very cordial and cooperative, but as the days wore on the competitive spirit of Marciano began to emerge and he began to snort fire through some of the sequences, especially when the script called for him to corner Ali and wing to the body.

The Krupp gun body attack of Marciano was his strength in the ring and the old faded experts of the many gyms throughout the country kept shifting their cigars nervously in speculation of what Marciano would have done to the young Clay kid with his body attack. The Frazier fights and the Foreman fight were in the future and no one could anticipate Ali's innate toughness, and his ability to take body punishment while inflicting his own lethal punishment.

Finally one hot afternoon Marciano, never known for his pinpoint accuracy, let go a few howitzer shots which caught Ali unaware since they were pulling their punches for the camera, and the resounding thumps could be heard all the way to the street. Ali gasped and sank to one knee, while Rocky pulled off, chagrined and embarrassed by his lack of control in the heat of simulated battle. Rocky's juices were working and Ali seemed to see the old champion in a new light and with renewed respect. In passing, I might add my own personal observation; with both in their prime, Ali would have destroyed Rocky, which is not to demean the Rock's considerable talents. However, his was a talent to absorb punishment while waiting to dispense his own bad medicine to the opponent. Ali would have been too fast, too smart, too big, and too much for Rocky's sensitive facial tissues, which were inordinately frail for a boxer whose style was to catch every punch in the face. I do not maintain that it might not have been the fight of his lifetime, but Ali would have stopped Rocky. Later Joe Frazier was to come to the top of the heap with the same style of fighting, but with good facial tissue, and absorb three of the biggest beatings I have ever seen inflicted on a fighter, for one cannot escape the axiom of the Fifth Street Gym: *The bigger they are, the bigger the beating!*

During the fight Ali worked his particular kind of personality magic on Woroner. Everyone who works with Ali comes out convinced that he is one of the few people who is his true friend, and that Ali hangs on every word of solicited or unsolicited advice. He has a little-boy way of asking pertinent questions about his co-worker's professional life as well as private life, giving off cute inside bits of information that the man feels he is privileged to hear for the first time. The net result is a dyed-in-the-wool friend and fan for life. Murray Woroner fell into this trap and came away from the filming with the feeling that he had Ali in his hip pocket, and all that was needed was to find a way to get him a license in order to put together an Ali revival which would make them both rich. As always, in these dog days, Ali would smile serenely and assure him that *he* was Ali's *main man,* and that anything he could do would be agreeable to Ali.

The plan of distribution left a lot to be desired since it was imperative that absolute secrecy be maintained. If the result of the fight was known, it robbed one of the pleasure of suspense. The film was distributed to all parts of the country and the world with rigid restrictions which predictably broke down as the foreign countries got the prints and preran the last round for purposes of making a few bucks, or for the simple pleasure of being the first to know. Whatever the reason, the fight was not a "betting" fight and the ending was so inflammatory that different sections of the world had different endings.

A word here before we leave this strange chapter of Ali's life in exile. This simulated fight was actually better than a real fight, and the audiences were on their feet halfway through the match cheering and rooting, and in the end they were almost in a frenzy. The fight was very well filmed, the sound effects and commentary added to the excitement, and the makeup was superb.

I sat in the Miami Beach Auditorium watching the effects on the audience with utter disbelief. When Marciano sustained a deep gash over his eye and the bright red makeup blood began to cover his upper torso, the crowd responded as they do in a real fight, some covering their eyes, most yelling for Ali to go to the eye, open it up more, and finish Rocky. After the fight I was repeatedly asked by members of the audience how bad was the cut and how many sutures I needed to close the cut. They seemed genuinely disappointed to learn that it was all make-believe, and that the blood was makeup. Strange people, fight fans. To this day, making after-dinner speeches, I usually show Ali's two fights with Liston, and as a teaser add one action-packed round of the Ali-Marciano computer fight. I have never had an audience that didn't prefer the computer fight to the other two for sheer excitement. I remain convinced Murray Woroner produced a minor masterpiece in this unique film. How was he to know it would cause him to have a coronary and lose a lot of sleep by the time the world got through with him.

Now flash forward to the year Ali makes his comeback and fights six successful fights. He has been assigned a black writer, Richard Durham, who is, was, could be, should be (depending on whom you talk to) a Black Muslim, and a past editor of the Muslim newspaper, *Muhammad Speaks*. Richard Durham is a small rotund man who looks nervous for the very sound reason that he is nervous. But he has the patience of a good writer and is the greatest collector of Ali stories on the face of the earth, bar none. To him fell the task of writing Ali's autobiography, *The Greatest*. As it turned out, he made a four-year career out of assimilating this data, in the course of which he insinuated himself into various deals, par for the Ali Circus, and not looked upon with disapproval. At this point in Ali's comeback Durham was digging into the past and talking to all and sundry, and when the stories dragged, he was not above staging an incident to get ammunition for the book; and so it is we come now to the Massacre of South Miami.

I had attempted to be as helpful as possible to Durham and Ali. The problem of the moment was that Durham wanted to interview Murray Woroner concerning the Marciano computer fight and was having some difficulty in arranging this interview, possibly because of Ali's role in sinking the Great Woroner Scheme for Cornering the Boxing Market, which I will describe shortly. I phoned Murray and arranged to bring the twosome out to see him on a sunny Saturday afternoon at his beautiful South Miami home. I understood that this was to be a friendly reunion, a rehashing of a commercially and artistically successful venture. Old friends reunited, a few old cuts touched up, a steak, and over and out.

As we were about to enter the Woroner domicile, Ali turned to me and said, "Stay out of this, Doc. I don't want you involved in this on tape," and I got that old sinking feeling in my stomach.

The door opened and Murray, looking thin and fit after his heart attack, greeted us in his effusive manner. His loyal and loving wife immediately made plans to go to the market and purchase the huge steaks she knows Ali loves, and we settled down to the interview. Woroner was ebullient, Ali subdued, and Durham began the interview with the same grim determination the Israeli prosecutor had at the Eichmann trials. Murray laughed and gave a flip answer. Durham feverishly pounded the line of questioning that led to the conclusion that the computer fight was a gigantic racist conspiracy devised by the whites of America to discredit the image of a great black champion (Ali)! *Who* were these judges on the panel that fed the computer the information? Where was the computer? *Birmingham! Aha, crackerland, USA.* Who read and interpreted the readouts? Who wrote the scripts? Who shot it? Who distributed it? And at the end of each question the inevitable: *Were they white or black men?*

By this time Murray Woroner was getting somewhat steamed. In all his years as a registered rebel and liberal he had never been accused of racism. He fought very hard to do the computer fight which gave Ali some financial ease at a time when money was scarce and, more important, kept his name before the public in a socially acceptable fashion. Now both Durham and Ali were using the word "nigger" over and over, which offended Murray, and he attempted to stop this runaway railroading by becoming indignant and forbidding *them* to use the word "nigger" in *his* house. He told them it was one of the few words forbidden in his house in front of his small children and he would not have Ali, who was a hero to his children, defiling the hearth even if he was the "main nigger" in the world. I was off to the side regarding all of this in open-mouthed amazement, and I saw through the kitchen window Murray's faithful wife doing a flamenco on the steaks, screaming, "Get those bums out of my house . . . get them out . . . out . . . out."

Finally the racist tidal wave abated and we were ushered out into the bright sunshine of a beautiful Florida afternoon. Ali seemed serenely peaceful and he put his arm around Murray, who was on his fifth nitroglycerine sublingual tablet, clutching his heart and grasping his chest. Easily, slipping into his Uncle Tom imitation, Ali said, "Boss-man, how about a hundred advance on my royalties?"

From the kitchen comes a stifled Jewish seagull shriek. *"Give him nothing . . . Murray . . . give him nothing."*

The sound is finally drowned out by the sound of demolished steaks going into the garbage disposal. Murray, actually going through his pockets, says apologetically, "Sorry, Ali, I don't carry that kind of money in my shorts."

We get into the car and roar sheepishly off, and it is well into the ride before Durham breaks the silence. "See, Ali, this is the type of controversial stuff we need for the book."

It is to Durham's final credit, or Random House's, or Ali's, that this material was not used in the book, although the theory of the white conspiracy and the computer discreditability was used. At last report, Murray is busy computerizing Golda Meir's hyperthyroidism and its relation to the Six-Day War, as a safer alternative than messing with the fight game.

The other event which caused Ali to come to the sobering realization that fighting was his identity and his life was the abortive attempt to have him star in a Broadway show.

The play *Big Buck White* had been an off-Broadway success, and it occurred to a talented and innovative producer, Zev Bufman, to produce this show as a musical with music by Oscar Brown, Jr., and a cast of tough black professionals, and have as the main character an amateur, Muhammad Ali.

The rehearsals were a shambles, but by opening night Ali had responded like the champion he is and was outdoing the professionals. Opening night was truly a happening.

Zev Bufman had hand-picked a hip, shrewd audience of people sympathetic to the black cause, and Bufman recalls it was a brilliant hit on the first night. Backers materialized from everywhere with fistfuls of money and checks for a piece of the action. Zev smiled politely and turned them all down. It was the beginning of the greying of his head.

Ali, used to personal highs of one night, could not respond with the steady professional performance needed night after night. By the end of a few nights, Zev wisely saw the handwriting on the wall and regretfully closed the show. Never in the history of Broadway had a show had such acclaim on opening night and closed so precipitously the following week.

Bufman, fully recovered from the shock of turning down so much backer money, and then closing a show and taking a heroic-size financial bath, now looks at the experience with the bemused outlook of a man who survived a torpedoing during the war. Besides Ali's flat performance after the opening night high, the backstage wars with the militant blacks threatened to close the show as well as burn the building, and throw in the producer for good measure. In looking back over these harrowing weeks, Bufman recalls that Ali was the peacemaker. Ali is an innately peaceful man, full of fun and love, and he used his position with the hard, professional blacks to cool them off and bring some semblance of order to an otherwise chaotic situation.

I went to see Ali on the last night, and felt that it was indeed a good thing that the play was closing. He seemed out of place and uncomfortable in his role, and although he had control when he was "on," he seemed totally out of it when the action did not involve him, which is one of the marks of an amateur onstage. Backstage, in his dressing room, he received me in his usual funny manner, rolling his eyes, as he does when he wants people to think he is amazed by some unusual thing. "Ain't this sumptin, Doc, ain't this *sumptin?*"

Zev Bufman still looks at this disaster and feels something good came out of it: a warm and personal friendship with Muhammad Ali. He feels Ali was very cooperative, friendly, and protective, and that they would never have made opening night but for Ali's peacekeeping involvement.

I was happy to see him out of that disaster, and happiest to know that Ali had reaffirmed his knowledge that he was best suited for the ring, casting aside his theatrical pretensions. Ali can be good only when he is interpreting a role as himself—when he is playing Ali. That is not a bad way to be a movie actor when you have a strong, likable personality like Ali. After all, it is a style that has served several people pretty well. Like Gable, Cooper, Monroe, Taylor, and so on forever.

6·Murray Woroner
and the Impossible Dream

Some time after Murray Woroner finished the Ali-Marciano Computer fight, an idea was born in his head that he could put together a comeback fight for Ali, and somewhere along the way become famous and wealthy. As happens to people working with Ali for the first time, he had fallen under Ali's spell. When Ali left Miami he left with Woroner the strong impression that Ali was one of his best friends and that it was incumbent on Woroner to devise a way to get him a fight in spite of the public feeling that Ali not only should not be allowed to fight, but should be in jail for his draft-dodging stance.

Ali had been denied the right to fight in every state in the Union; however, every state had its own boxing commission, and most states had no boxing commission, since boxing is seen only in several states in the Union on a regular basis. Murray Woroner had done his homework and found that Florida had a gigantic loophole.

Murray's plan had several stages, each dependent on the other in sequential steps, and began with the most elemental step: Get Muhammad Ali a license in Florida. This accomplished, he had to get the two existing champions to agree to fight him in an elimination tournament. The WBA champion, based on an eight-fighter elimination tournament, was Jimmy Ellis, who was managed by Angelo Dundee, and who was very close to me. The New York champion was Smoking Joe Frazier, managed by the Cloverlay group out of Philadelphia. He had to get them to agree to fight in unusual surroundings: a sound stage in south Florida. The details of this were remarkable, and I will explain them at length in a moment, for they demonstrate how far the human imagination can soar when released from the bounds of standard operating procedures.

Three or four highly profitable fights would have resulted from tying up the three existing champions, even more so if the fights proved close and controversial, which would mean a series of rematches. Was this a pipe dream? Did it have a chance? Or was Woroner, as the pundit of the Fifth Street Gym is fond of saying, just jerking off? Well, let's see.

The first hurdle appeared the hardest. All the sharp people in boxing were trying to get Ali a license and failing miserably because of his unpopular position. Politicians loved to get into the act by turning Ali down, adding luster to their records by opposing his right to earn a living while his case was still in the courts. They would dwell with senile rapture on the virtuous records of past champions (forgetting the remarkable war records of Jack Dempsey, Sugar Ray Robinson, Rocky Graziano, etc.) and vilify Ali, thereby adding uncounted voters to their roll. The hurdle defied the efforts of the best minds in boxing. Harold Conrad, a knowledgeable boxing entrepreneur, ex–movie writer, ex–sports-writer, and a mover in things political, had exhausted all efforts to subvert some politician to his way of thinking, and was at the end of the tether. Bob Arum, a sharp young lawyer out of Louis Nizer's law firm, had gotten fairly rich from being Ali's attorney and had excellent political connections around the country, but had exhausted his possibilities. Out-of-the-country promoters were discounted, since the State

Department would not permit Ali out of the country to fight. It appeared that for the moment the Ali Circus was side-tracked. They had not counted on the guile of Murray Woroner.

In studying the laws of the State of Florida, Woroner correctly perceived that each boxing commission was autonomous in its own locale. The governor had no say-so in its makeup or regulations. It was solely responsible to its sponsoring group. The sponsors could only be several organizations which profited from each fight, and they were usually veterans' organizations like the VFW. The road looked clear to Woroner. First he would go to an obscure township in south Florida and convince the mayor by means of judicious contributions to his favorite fund (himself) to appoint a boxing commission, which was an easy first step. The mayor would agree and appoint his brother and two other relatives as the boxing commission. Their first and only official act was to issue Ali a license to fight in their locale. Done. The governor would be powerless to stop them, but the next step would be harder. How are you going to get a veterans' organization to approve Ali, draft dodger? Here I was called into the fray. I had the connection in Tampa to impose on an old friendship and get the vets' group there to sponsor the South Miami Commission. This they would do for the nominal fee of five hundred dollars. Woroner agreed to pay the five hundred dollars, and we were in business with a boxing commission approving, a vets' group blessing, and a governor powerless to stop the fight. It appeared that we were on the way. This little ploy cost me a good friend in that Woroner never paid the five hundred dollars, but that is not an unusual story in boxing, and to be fair the entire Alice in Wonderland adventure cost Murray Woroner considerable money, as we shall see.

The next stage was to get an arena in that locale big enough to house the fight. Big enough or *small enough,*

Murray said with Cheshire cat smile. The whole thing was getting curiouser and curiouser. Woroner had leased an old sound stage used to make small films for commercial purposes. His plan was to isolate this building and have the fight filmed, *without public present*. It would take two weeks to process the film and distribute it throughout the world. At a precise date, all cans of film would be open and it would be shown throughout the world simultaneously. First, the publicity would be staggering, and the security measures would have to be of CIA-FBI magnitude. Second, the entire crew had to agree to be locked up in the studio, incommunicado, for the two weeks it would take to process and distribute the film. This would entail quite an operation since both fighters, their handlers, the officials, camera crews, and service people would come to at least *thirty* people. One slip of the lip, and the profits would evaporate before our eyes. Can you imagine Ali and Frazier locked up in the studio for two weeks following their first fight? What if one fighter sustained a serious injury requiring hospitalization? No newsmen were to be allowed in, and this could backfire and cause the fight to be ignored by the press. A fate worse than death.

But Murray Woroner was prepared to go to extreme lengths to insure the comfort of the participants. All in all, he was going to have quite a diverse group to house and feed.

Murray was finally convinced that this was the way to have the fight and avoid the political fights, as well as the adverse public reaction in that small south Florida hamlet. By the time anyone knew what we were doing, the fight would be in the can. The publicity accruing would be a natural, and when all was said and done, Ali would be back in action and the subsequent fights would be easy and could be done in more orthodox fashion. As it turned out in Atlanta, that is exactly what happened. Once Ali got back to fighting, the rest of the nation fell into place and permitted him to fight without further hoo-haa.

The question of financing now came into play. Thinking ahead, Murray began to think of how to get the proper funds to pull off the first fight. He estimated he needed at least one million dollars. He saw no possibility of any normal, conservative money men advancing that kind of money for this kind of bizarre adventure. While this problem might be foremost, it was obviously necessary to sign the fighters before he could go after the money.

Jimmy Ellis was the WBA champion and a sweetheart of a man. A quiet family man, he knew he needed just so many fights to accumulate enough money to bring up his large family and have some financial security. His manager was Angelo Dundee, who had brilliantly engineered Jimmy into the heavyweight elimination by virtue of a stunning one-round upset of a Madison Square Garden favorite son, light-heavyweight Jimmy Pearsol. Then, the decided underdog in all his fights, Jimmy Ellis took on the top three heavyweights and beat them all, stopping Leotis Martin in the first round, decisioning Oscar Bonavena, and outthinking Jerry Quarry using a brilliant fight plan devised by the crafty Angelo Dundee. Ellis was a good fighter.

Smoking Joe Frazier had all the earmarks of a great fighter as he came up from the streets of Philadelphia under the stern leadership of Yancey Durham and the benevolent financial leadership of the Cloverlay group. Yancey knew that Joe was not quite ready to step into the competition of the elimination tournament, and so he refused to allow Joe to participate. Then, when the smoke cleared and Ellis was declared champion, Yancey and the New York sharpshooters devised a phony heavyweight title encompassing three states, creating a division in the heavyweight ranks and spurring a demand for an Ellis-Frazier fight. By this time Frazier was ready to face anyone, but he really wanted Ali, who would forever overshadow him. Frazier was a great fighter.

Muhammad Ali was a legend by now, but his ring rust

would be evident. First he would have to fight Ellis, against whom he had the best chance. This would create strange problems, since Angelo and I worked with both fighters. That could be settled in this manner: Angelo was Ellis' manager and Ali's trainer. The financial position precluded all else—Angelo would have to work with Ellis. I would be the doctor for both, so I could avoid working in either corner. (Ali was ready to fight without *any* cornermen if necessary.) Ali was a super great fighter.

Ellis signed immediately, although Angelo was not so happy about the arrangement. This would almost surely guarantee Ellis at least two fights and maybe a third. Win or lose, Ellis would be home free as far as the money was concerned.

We had to go to Philadelphia to talk to the austere attorney for Cloverlay, Bruce Wright, and the flamboyant Yank Durham. The mild incongruity of sitting at an old-line Philadelphia club talking about a distasteful subject like a boxing tournament between three black fighters, one of them a draft dodger, in the shadow of Independence Hall, was not lost on me. Added to that were the wildly divergent sartorial styles displayed by Bruce, in tweed jacket and button-down shirt, thin tie, short pants, and cordovan wingtip shoes, and Murray Woroner in Miami Beach wheeler-dealer duds with patent red shoes and maroon suit. Seeing Murray served a chicken salad sandwich on white toast with mayonnaise, and looking at the expression of disbelief and distaste on his face, was worth the uncomfortable trip. In the end we signed Joe Frazier.

On our way back to New York by train, Murray was ecstatic. The hard part was out of the way. Ali remained to be signed, but he took this for granted since this whole thing was for Ali's benefit. I nodded absently and cringed inside. Obviously he didn't know Ali, a man of a million surprises. Still, two out of three wasn't a bad week's work.

I found myself irretrievably enmeshed in helping Murray make this dream come true, and although I had seen too much of boxing to think that it would happen as he thought it would, I felt it could be accomplished with some compromises.

Murray would have to turn to the boxing establishment for help. In a closed group like the boxing fraternity there is a common axiom: *Screw the newcomer.* They have no board to prevent anyone from promoting boxing or getting into the business of boxing, but they do have a wagon-train-closed-ring approach to defend their control of the game. It is a matter of mutual protection, which I fully understand, but Murray Woroner, flushed with these repeated early successes, and already savoring the fruits of impending financial profit, would not listen to my strong warnings.

At this point in the operation, if Murray Woroner would have turned to older and wiser boxing heads and included them in the operation, even if in a minor capacity, I am convinced he would have pulled it off. I pleaded with him to include Chris Dundee, the long-time successful promoter of boxing in Miami, to get the best boxing legal mind in Bob Arum, to hire a go-getter like Harold Conrad, to go to an international promoter like Jarvis Astaire to facilitate world-wide distribution, but Murray turned a deaf ear to these entreaties since he had already given away points in his promotion to unimportant co-workers who could not help him and were of no importance to the promotion, except as interested spectators. His attorney was a very capable man in Miami, but this was his first exposure to the world of boxing on an international scale, and he certainly couldn't know the angles like Bob Arum, who had learned how to fight in the dim, dark world of boxing business.

Murray was still thrashing about looking for the money when it occurred to me that no sane man would put up one million, but a gambler might, and so I called a long-time friend, Bob Martin, in Las Vegas. Bob is the acknowledged brain of the betting fraternity. He establishes the *line* every week, which is the very bottom line in making or breaking. He has been a very respectable citizen of Las Vegas for many years now, and his wisdom in the matter of sports events is well documented. He is especially sharp in boxing matters, and loved Ali from the time he was an amateur. Once he gave me the best piece of financial advice I ever got from anyone. When Ali was about to have his first fight Bob told me, "Bet on this kid until he loses and you will be a rich man." Martin was intrigued by this audacious scheme and referred me to Sid Wyman, the owner of the Dunes, who had the funds, the love of boxing, and the imagination it takes to put this much money on the line. His only condition was that we forget the movie idea and produce it as a closed-circuit fight. I breathed a sigh of relief, for the movie idea was the only part of this production that did not seem remotely feasible. Now we had a workable production, the money, and two out of the three champions signed. Back to the drawing board.

The new plan called for the fight to be held in the same studio and a blue-ribbon audience to be invited at one thousand dollars a seat, the proceeds to be donated to the Black Orphans of Vietnam Veterans. Go fight that.

And so Murray was cruising down the street of instant fame when a last-minute realization struck him: he had not signed Ali. Now began some Machiavellian machinations that still must seem inexplicable to Woroner. Ali began to procrastinate. Arum began to maneuver. The organization began to do its number, and suddenly Murray had troubles.

Ali felt, or was advised, that he could not put himself in the hands of this two-bit amateur from South Miami. Fun is fun, but when the chips are down the Big Boys should take over. Arum saw to it that Ali signed nothing without his advice, and other plans were cooking that would include the boxing crowd. Still there was time to restructure the deal and include Arum and the sharp boys of boxing, but Murray still thought he had it locked up with two out of three fighters signed and the money guaranteed, and so he sent his attorney to New York to deal with Arum for Ali's services.

To send this capable but inexperienced man to deal with Arum was like sending Mark Spitz to fight the shark in *Jaws*. No contest. Arum actually had him come to the office and wait in the outside room while he took care of some business details. The only problem was that the business details were in Tampa, Florida, about a thousand miles away. Yes, he sat in the outside waiting room while Arum sped to Tampa to structure a similar deal in Tampa with a fly-by-night promoter trying to imitate Woroner's deal. At this point the entire transaction, so close to fruition, dissolved in a comic opera series of deals, double deals, double crosses, and verbiage. Bottom line, Ali went to Atlanta, Georgia, of all places, and began the second half of his remarkable career.

Every time I see Woroner these days I shake my head. If only he would have included the right people, we would have written a remarkable chapter in the already bizarre history of boxing, but I find that it is very hard for people to grasp the simple facts of life when they are so close to the goal line.

PART THREE

The Comeback

7·Prelude to Disaster

The dusty dressing room in Miami was stuffy and smelled of rancid socks as Ali walked in with Richard Durham, his Boswell of the past eighteen months. Ali was dressing in his boxing gear when he turned to me and asked when I was going to New York for the medical exam prior to the Frazier fight. I was taken aback because we were to have flown together after the Ellis-Doyle fight that night. He blithely informed me that he and Durham were going after the gym workout that afternoon because they had to work on their picture deal; they would meet us in New York on Wednesday. These abrupt changes in Ali's plans were no surprise to me, but it was a taste of more things to come. Angelo walked in and took the news in his usual unflappable style.

The Ellis fight went off without a hitch, Ellis winning big with a ten-round KO, Angelo and I not having to work very hard. The next morning we awoke early and boarded a plane with Budd Schulberg who was down to cover the end of the training camp. On the plane we discussed the thought-out and agreed-upon plan of doing the exam and returning to Miami for the last three days of training, then flying back to New York. Angelo wanted Ali under no circumstances to stay in New York City and be exposed to crowd pressures and the exigencies of the press. John X. Condon, publicity director of the Garden, had gone over Angelo's head to Herbert and gotten Ali booked for the Carson show that night, which was against Angelo's expressed desires. But, as in every transaction, nothing would be resolved until we talked to Ali that morning and got his reaction.

Angelo, Budd, and I arrived at the Hilton and had to cool our heels in the lobby for fifteen minutes until Ali and Durham finished transacting their independent movie business. This bears taking a look at for the purpose of understanding the confusion in the camp, with many factions pulling in separate directions for their own gain.

Jerry Perenchio and Jack Kent Cooke had signed Muhammad Ali to a contract for all of his services for two-and-a-half million dollars. This would include everything connected with the fight, a point that was later violently debated. One of Perenchio's main projects was a documentary film to be made during the training period, the fight, and the postfight period. Richard Durham had a contract to do the Ali life story in book form, and that was to be made into a film. Somewhere along the line C. B. Atkins and Durham came up with the idea to produce their own documentary, and entered feverish negotiations with an independent group of film makers. By this time only a week or two of training remained. Durham and Ali then banned Perenchio's film makers from the gym. For a week they killed time at the door of the gym, filming door knobs and car trunks and the mob scene outside. Finally, the showdown came between Perenchio and Durham.

They met in the gym, in the small cubicle Ali used as a private exercise room. No one was present except Ali, who lay on the rubbing table quiet and inert, resting while the argument raged on above his chest. Perenchio spoke long and loud about Ali's obligations to him and to Cooke. Durham heatedly replied, "This ain't no Plantation Deal, you don't get the house, the field hands and all the cotton for that two-and-a-half million."

"We got a contract for this," Perenchio said, pointing to Ali's chest.

Ali remained motionless, following the argument with his eyes only. It was the one time I have ever witnessed Ali uninvolved in an argument relating to him or his business.

"I was there when you signed the contract and we specifically mentioned his being able to do other things." Durham was coldly pointing out his unwillingness to permit Ali to become an indentured slave.

Perenchio took a long hard look at Durham and tersely, nose to nose, barked at him, "Who the f— are *you?* I haven't seen you at any contract talks or signings. What gives you the right to talk for *him?*" Again pointing at the recumbent form of Ali.

The meeting broke down into name calling, and the end result was that no one reached an agreement.

Despite this, Perenchio's camera crews, idle outside the gym, were once again permitted inside to resume shooting and recording every event large or small that occurred inside Chris Dundee's Fifth Street Gym. Durham's negotiations continued, overlapping into the New York Hilton for a final signing. Soon it was Wednesday, March 3, and the fight was only five days away. If these people had been serious about doing a documentary of our fistic Woodstock, they certainly blew the best opportunities by their endless negotiations which took up and exhausted Ali's time. The one commodity that Ali could not spare was time: time to prepare and time to store up his energies for the terrible test to come. He was dissipating time and strength in useless negotiations for a film deal that might never come off.

Budd Schulberg was with us on this part of the trip and his help was sought by the film makers. Budd's reputation is international as a writer and film maker, and his *The Harder They Fall* is probably one of the finest boxing movies that has been made. His biggest kick is following the fight game, and because of our growing friendship I was determined that he see the inside of this situation. His help as an advisor had been sought by Durham, who was having second thoughts about this, since the disorganization was apparently going to lead to a fiasco that might sap the champ's energies.

The door of the suite opened to reveal a few figures in huddled conversation, among them the huge figure of the champ. A slight, oily-looking, balding man came forth extending a wet clammy hand. His shingle-salesman approach put me off immediately, and he did not counteract this initial impression with the nonstop dialogue that followed. He prefaced his remarks with the disclaimer that he was not a film man, per se, but a lawyer who was involved in multi-million-dollar deals throughout the world. When the sums reached astronomical heights and outraced believability, I edged out of the conversation, leaving him to direct his non-stop assault on the credibility gap at courteous Budd Schulberg, who was staring at him, transfixed by his cobra eyes and machine-gun delivery.

The final signing had taken place, but with no arrangement for the shooting of the film, which was a shame because the best Woodstock actions were to follow in a few minutes. Their idea of filming took place in Miami over the following two days, when they shot stereotyped scenes like the one where Reggie and Ali venture forth with the following inspired dialogue.

Reggie: "What are you going to do with your house in Philly?"

Ali: "I think I will give it to my folks, they deserve a good house after all of these years."

Reggie: "That is great, Champ."

The mind boggles at the real drama constantly swirling around Ali that would make great footage, and at the waste of film that results in acted-out scenes such as these. Those film makers ended up by asking Ali what film *he* wanted to shoot, which is roughly like the doctor asking the patient where the patient wants him to cut. It served no purpose other than to occupy the champ's mind and exhaust him in details that he should not have been bothered with in the first place. A fighter should concentrate on the fight, and no more. Period.

The movie episode temporarily out of the way, Ali decided to worry about the Johnny Carson show, and said he was going to stay in New York until the fight. Angelo paled. He envisioned the energy-draining mob scenes in the streets of New York, and the pulling and pushing of the press. Frazier had gone home to Philly and the press would be at a loss as to what to write while awaiting the fight. They would be all over Ali, as usual.

But Angelo wisely rolled with the punch and decided to wait and convince Ali later. In this contradictory frame of mind, we moved on to Madison Square Garden and the physical examination.

A full battery of reporters and photographers awaited the champion's entrance. Soon Ali swaggered into view and a hum of expectation arose from the hardened veterans of the news media. Ali is always news, and great copy. Today was to prove no exception.

Doing what amounted to a half-hour chunk of comic material, Ali easily dominated the session. That would have made a great documentary if anyone had been around to shoot it. He did a two-man act with the doctor who kept admonishing him to "be serious." Irrepressible Ali, the imp, kept up a rapid-fire monologue worthy of a top-flight comedian. At one point in the interview, a Roumanian reporter, reading laboriously from a prepared statement, handed him a doll from Roumania, and Ali graciously accepted and continued the interview for a few minutes, then realized he was being photographed with the doll and handed it to Bundini, saying, "Here, take this, it don't look good for the Heavyweight Champion of the World to be playing with dolls."

Back in the dressing room, plans were being laid by Condon to keep Ali in New York. He was to exercise, box, have a fifteen-minute press conference, and then retire to the dressing room to sleep for a few hours so that the crowds below would disperse. This was the plan, but the next few minutes would destroy it.

To begin with, the dressing room began to fill to astonishing proportions with all sorts of people. Burt Lancaster and Don Dunphy were to do the color and commentary on the fight, and they brought in their people as well as a flood of fans. Bundini brought in his strange people off the streets, and assorted Muslims began to filter in. In no time, it became apparent that the Garden wasn't going to be any place to relax in, and egress from it became a really serious problem. A clot of ugly people had begun to form outside. Condon, the security people, and our crowd started to plot some way to escape.

Ali began to see the wisdom of Angelo's thoughts. Soon we agreed on a plan wherein the limousine would pull up into the Garden on an inside ramp, load up, and escape before the crowds would know what was happening. Alas, we underestimated the sensitive radar of that most frightening of all human elements, the Mob.

We stood awaiting the limo, Ali hidden from sight. Soon it churned up the steep incline. The smooth purring of the Cadillac engine was complemented by the growing growling of the crowd. The limo was pulling a comet of human satellites. We dove for the limo and they dove for us. The fight for the doors began. Budd had the outside front door. He found it hard to close, but soon, although trembling from the exertion and anxiety of the moment, he was able to close the door. An assortment of followers jumped inside the car with us, and we raced off into cross-town traffic. Well, not exactly raced off—we hit eighteen traffic lights in a row, all red.

The hardier members of the mob raced alongside the Caddy, pounding its sides and hollering at Ali. It was a display of affection, but frightening all the same. One pimple-faced white kid with long hippie hair and a World War II jacket was the hardiest of the lot. He stuck to us for a few miles, until finally Ali good-naturedly rolled down the window and shook his hand.

"Man, you sumptin else," Ali laughed.

Finally, his energy used up and his sneaker blown out, the kid quit, waving a tired hand, and struggled to the curb like an exhausted miler.

Now all was silent in the limo as we rolled off toward the airport. Ali was not contradicting Angelo now. Everyone agreed his judgment was correct: to stay in this town would be a disaster. Still Ali was not through. In the rear seat, sitting next to him, was a brother from Philadelphia—Jeremiah. His personal desire was to see Ali in Philly for the next three days and, coincidentally, hitch a ride home to Philly. Ali had just bought a home in Philly and the idea appealed to him, especially the part of being able to bug Frazier in his gym. Psychological warfare was Ali's specialty, and he had a few tricks thought up for the serious Frazier.

We arrived at the airport in horrible weather. The field was rapidly being socked in, and this did not heighten Ali's desire to take a long trip to Miami. Confusion reigned. Angelo validated his four tickets to Miami.

Ali vacillated. He turned to me. "Doc, you haven't seen my house in Cherry Hill and my Rolls. You got to come with us and stay at my house."

Three days in Philly is life in Yuma in my book, but I acquiesced. It's hard to turn this guy down.

"Find out what he wants to drive us the ninety miles to Philly."

"Fifty cents a mile," the chauffeur states.

"Offer him two hundred," says Ali, doing some fast mental calculations.

Then hunger overcame him and he noticed a group of people at the door of the fancy restaurant in the terminal. It was the colored staff of the restaurant, offering him their services. This sounded good and he moved in to the table to sit down with his eight people. Still no decision, and the last call for the plane sounded on the terminal intercom. Angelo moved to the edge of Ali's chair, four tickets to Miami spread out like a poker hand. Indecision prevailed. Butter, water, bread were placed before eight people. Still no move. Primary thinking is going on in Ali's head. Let me eat, *then* I'll make the decision.

Bingham, the photographer, comes to the rescue with the information that the stewardesses aboard the jet are warming up *two* steaks for the champion with some nice fresh vegetables. Ali arises. Situation in hand at last. It's back to Miami through the raging storm. Sorry about that, restaurant brothers. So Angelo finally wins, but by a close split decision.

Now the fight is only two days off and, after quite a bit of confusion at the Garden, I got John X. Condon to get Harry Markson to agree on two limousines to pick up Ali and his crew as they arrived that night at Kennedy. Since Ali had picked the New Yorker Hotel for its proximity to the Garden, we were stuck with it, and the security people were no happier than I, since the New Yorker was jammed with, of all things, a shoe convention. The lobby was crowded with shoe distributors from Muncie and Duluth. But we managed to arrange to have a back elevator working solely for us, and rooms were assigned to all the members of the entourage. The cool efficiency of the hotel staff was admirable to observe.

I was instructed to call John Ali, the Muslim in charge of arrangements at the St. Regis. I noted idly that the executive branch of this outfit had better sense than to stay at the New Yorker. He was unavailable all day, but I ran into Chauncey Eskridge, Ali's attorney, outside the New Yorker giving a television interview to some Italian television people, and was able to inform him that I had two limos going to the airport, and not to send other people at the last minute.

The preparations over, I left for the airport with Dr. Gus Moreno, a New York gynecologist, in one limo and me in the other. As we awaited the arrival of the jet we plotted a getaway before the everpresent crowds would be able to form. Gus was to handle the baggage and the entourage at the lower level, and I was to whisk Ali, Angelo, Durham, and Bundini to the upper ramp limo for a fast takeoff. But, seconds later, news photographers arrived along with two more limos that Ali had ordered; inside them were Bingham's brother from the coast and a stewardess girl friend. Nothing is ever simple. Utilizing our added transport, we rearranged our convoy just as Ali was disembarking. I managed to steer Ali into the upper ramp limo and all of his followers attempted to jam in so that, instead of a comfortable six passengers and driver, we had ten people and some hand luggage, with three semiempty limos trailing behind us. At the hotel all was in readiness and, thankfully, there was no foulup so that the champ went to bed peacefully before his entourage and twenty-seven pieces of luggage arrived.

Sunday, March 7, 1971, passed quietly until three in the afternoon when Ali decided to see a few of the press. I went down and rounded up Budd, Jim Murray, Jose Torres, and a few others, and Ali began a three-hour talkathon that was amusing and served to expel nervous energies that he felt. The culmination was an hour special on Joe Frazier which gave him added vigor and humor as he invented special material about his adversary.

One particular bit stuck in my mind. As he got up to leave the room, bare-chested and in stockinged feet, he sneered at Joe Frazier's show business aspirations.

"No big man can play love scenes with itty-bitty girls and say (here in a low rumbling voice) 'I LOVES YOU.' . . . You need a small, neat, compact man to say that, 'I LOVE YOU UUUUUUUUUUU.' "

The day before the weigh-in, John X. Condon and I had gone through the steps needed to get Ali into the Garden without a riot. We decided that the same Greek limo chauffeur would pick us up on the Eighth Avenue side of the New Yorker after exiting from the rear of the building, drive directly to the Thirty-third Street ramp of the Garden, where four cops and a wooden barricade would cut off the following crowd, and zoom up the five-flight ramp to the dressing-room level. Once there, the police and security people would keep strangers out. Then, following the weigh-in, we would adjourn to the upper levels and hide, Phantom-of-the-Opera style, until fight time. John promised a comfortable bed, color TV, and a phone for Ali's peace of mind. The plan looked foolproof. Alas, things don't always work out the way they are planned. Especially in Ali's camp.

The arrangement of the hideout proved questionable. That was to be settled later, and it was decided not to tell Ali about it until after the weigh-in since he would undoubtedly change his mind four times before we settled on the final answer.

The exit was accomplished with a minimum of difficulties. As usual, several more people than were counted on crammed into the limo with us, so that I had Bundini and his gear on my lap. Since the trip was literally just crossing the street, I laughed. Then, slowly, as the Greek drove by the Thirty-third Street ramp, it occurred to me that we were locked into another Keystone Kops chase. Thirty-third Street is one way and the Greek decided to go around the Garden, which is surrounded by one-way streets, which means Magellan would have had a tough time making it without going in circles. At this time a blue car passed us and waved good-naturedly. The Greek, inspired by this slight show of leadership, followed the car past the Thirty-third Street ramp a second time.

Bundini's weight was numbing my legs, and I yelled to the driver, "Where the hell are you going?"

"I am following the blue car," he answered, amazed at the question.

"What blue car! He isn't with us! He doesn't know where we are going!"

Another circuit and we finally imposed our collective wills upon the obtunded driver so he pulled into the Thirty-*fourth* Street ramp, which meant we had cleverly outflanked our barrier and police protection. That, it turned out, was just as well since, instead of the promised four husky young gendarmes, there was one old, semiretired minion of the law. The car ground to a halt before a ramp door that slowly opened to admit us and closed, castle-drawbridge fashion, sealing off the humanoids who discovered our presence, rushed after us with a collective roar, and swallowed the old policeman.

The weigh-in was the usual Ali shouting and jesting. Very satisfying to the public and newsmen. Celebrities in the crowd applauded and he took it all in his usual smiling stride. Just before the weigh-in he had done a bit in the dressing room for the closed-circuit TV cameras, opening an envelope and reading his prediction: *Frazier will go in six.* Lancaster, handsome in tuxedo, did the honors, and all went smoothly.

Following a relatively quiet exit to the hideout, we went into a conference. The three-circuit ride to the Garden had convinced Ali that the Mob was out there again, and to risk going back to the hotel, then back to the Garden was not necessary. We made for the room that we had designated as the hideout. True to Madison Square Garden form, we were locked out. After a long search for the key, we were let in. I already had my doubts about the room, but to confirm my worst fears I gave it a quick, intensive scanning as the lights went on. Sure enough: No TV, no phone, and nothing but a psychiatrist's small cot for a bed. Ali balked. I immediately phoned the Garden's Harry Markson, who went into a semi-spastic dance but produced a bed of sorts, which satisfied Ali but was really a folding bed that was not fit for a six-foot-three man to rest on. The friends of Ali, who number quite a few around fight time, gathered to keep him company in the other room. Not exactly what we had in mind, but Ali is different than other fighters in that respect. He needs company and likes to talk before a fight, when other fighters are sleeping and "getting themselves together."

At this time Ali remembered his old trainer, Fred Stoner. He had been asked to come to New York to work in Ali's corner, which displaced a valuable man, Chickie Ferrara. Stoner had started off the young Cassius Clay, but lost him to other boxing powers early in the game, and so, in a way, this was Ali's noble way of repaying him. It was noble but foolish in view of the fact that he was facing the most important test of his life against the strongest, toughest opponent he had ever faced. Since Stoner had never worked with Ali as a pro and was no longer particularly active in the sport, it was really giving a small edge to Frazier. When the going gets tough and the rounds late, it is very important to have active assistance from your corner to revive tired muscles and repair damage. Possibly Ali did not feel that the fight was going to go the limit or that he would need such assistance, or that the corner is important in a fight of this kind. Having worked a thousand fights, I feel an Angelo Dundee, a Chickie Ferrara, a Luis Sarria is a definite plus factor in the fighter's favor, especially in the late rounds when the minute repair job becomes an integral part of the picture.

Fight time found us ready to descend to dressing-room level. As we walked in, Ali caught sight of his brother fighting a Briton. It was a tough fight and close but Rahaman was losing, and Ali decided to stand and watch as he had the night of the Liston fight. It didn't do either one of them any good. Rahaman lost anyway, and Ali lost some more precious energy. Ali had always defied all of boxing's axioms, and he does not fret about conserving his energies, which prior to this had been boundless. But, then, he never had to face a human machine like Joe Frazier.

8·The First Frazier Fight

MARCH 8, 1971

Harry Markson came up to the assembled onlookers in the tunnel. A New York inspector was clutching his heart and his face was pale. He spoke to me. "Where is Angie? Where is Ali? It's forty-five minutes before fight time and he is not dressed . . . do you know why . . . because Bundini is outside with forty guys he wants let in without a ticket. . . . I can't do that. . . . I told them last time not to do this . . . we have laws . . . can't let in people . . . says he won't come in with the champ's equipment if we don't let him in."

Familiar with this ploy and sympathizing with the aggrieved Mr. Markson, we broached the subject gingerly to Ali, who didn't turn his head as he said, "Well, why don't you let them in?"

Markson fled in despair to renew the bickering with Bundini. Finally, as the minutes ticked off, he relented and compromised on letting in twelve of the brothers free. Bundini, smiling like a Cheshire cat, entered the dressing room with the equipment, and everyone breathed a sigh of relief.

Was there any need for the energy-sapping worry about

the brothers outside? Was it really Ali's business to worry about who gets in? What other champion was ever thus pre-occupied when he had infinitely more realistic things to worry about, namely, getting his rear end handed to him by the snorting bull, Joe Frazier. If he fights twenty more times Ali will always have someone at the door without the tickets. It's criminal to expect him to take on this additional burden.

Finally all preparations were out of the way, and in the nick of time we were ready to enter the arena. This is a moment hard to describe, but it surpassed any I've ever witnessed, including the first Liston fight. The Garden shook and the deafening roar was wildly more than I had antici-pated. They still loved Ali, the master showman. Frazier's entry was no less noisy. His supporters were highly vocal, and the bedlam that resulted was numbing.

Ali began a shadow-skipping step in ever widening circles, and soon he took off on a wide sweep of the ring, brushing past Joe Frazier, whispering the taunting word "chump," and laughing behind a pixyish smile. Even the solemn Smoking Joe Frazier had to smile. Now they were in the middle of the ring for instructions by Arthur Mercante. Ali continued to talk and jibe away at Joe, who returned taunts and alley threats in kind. Ali walked back to his corner and paused in a moment of silent Islamic prayer. Joe looked like a bulldog straining at the leash.

The corner was mobbed by Ali followers and camp people. The cornermen officially were Angelo Dundee, Fred Stoner, Bundini, Luis Sarria, and me. Each of us was avail-able for service if needed. Chickie Ferrara was sent to the opposite corner to observe, and we got the capable, friendly Gil Clancey in return from their corner. Reggie and Young-blood in tuxedos sat with us. Nearby Chris Dundee and Herbert sat in press seats. The usual early harassment by New York State officials began, but as the bout picked up in intensity the harassment abated spontaneously. After a few rounds the fighting mounted to a blistering pace and Budd Schulberg—rabid fight fan, rooter, and friend—could not stand the inactivity of the press section and joined us in the oddly caparisoned corner that mixed tuxedos with blood-red sweaters.

Behind us were Jack Kent Cooke's two rows, which included Andy Williams, Ethel Kennedy, Burt Bacharach, Senator Teddy Kennedy, Sargent Shriver, and the Cookes. That set was all for Ali, and as vocal as the peanut gallery, but in the ring it was a different story.

The highlights of the fight, in my mind, were these:

1. Ali winning the first two rounds but depressing me with the way he was missing Joe's bobbing head. The absence of Ali's prime weapon, the jab. He was very ineffective with it when he did land, and mainly he was hooking with a hooker, and that can be murder.

2. Smoking Joe winning the next two with the brute force of his attack. His face was amazing to watch. On defense he looked like King Kong beating off the ineffective bullets of the airplanes as he defied all mankind atop the Empire State Building, and then his face changed to sheer pleasure when he attacked with élan, *smiling* through blood-flecked mouthpiece, and taunting Ali. His devastating will to receive blows to return one or two effective punches. In the fourth round Joe is staggered by a beautiful combination, but fights his way out of it.

3. The first, sixth, seventh, eighth were notable for the continued blistering pace. In the minute between the first five rounds, Ali stood most of the time in the corner, but from here on in he sat. By the eighth round Ali had used all of his psychological ploys, to no avail. Here was the animal, at bay and dangerous, disregarding what Ali was doing in his single-minded desire to annihilate

his enemy. Ali in these rounds pursues a tricky course. He must rest from time to time. Previous to this he has bought time with a series of breathtaking tricks. Against Chuvalo he let his rival punch himself out, but to the body. Ali standing still on the ropes for two minutes at a time, ending up with an exhausted, dispirited Chuvalo, and a rested unhurt Ali. Frazier was not buying. He went to the attack, built up points, was not punched out, and hurt Ali, overlooking the fine psychological warfare. Against Liston, when blinded, Ali played with the lumbering Sonny, tapping his head lightly, forearm extended. This infuriated Liston and got his mind off the main mission, while chasing a shadow winded him. Frazier disregarded *anything* that Ali was doing. He was not reacting to Ali's jive, but orchestrating his own symphony. No matter what Ali did, Frazier was there with all of his considerable power and desire to win, chopping down and eroding all of Ali's gambits and strengths. Ali had to reach down into his trick bag for new tricks to confuse this one-track express train, but, alas, he had none, and his one great quality, his reflexes, were dulled by Father Time. Where once he slipped a punch by a whisker, now the punches were landing. Joe was doing his thing, left hooking with power, and Ali was not doing his, evading them. Therein lay the tale of the blackest round I have watched in a long time. The Gruesome Eleventh.

4. *Eleventh:* Joe and Ali were even up to this point: that is to say, if the fight had ended in ten I would have given it to Ali on rounds. However, a fifteen-round fight is considerably different, because a fighter is waging a longer, more tiring fight. Ali won a ten-round fight, but Frazier was winning a fifteen rounder at this point. All his things were working for him, and he was getting up a head of steam, whereas it seemed Ali was fading

in the late rounds. His fabulous legs and reflexes that had carried him out of range of the opponent's heavy artillery had suddenly begun to fail him, and the battering punches were not missing as much as they were landing. The playing on the ropes and pitty-patting punches had earned the scorn of Frazier, who correctly saw through the ruse, and had lost Ali at least three rounds, plus having given Frazier a chance to chastise the arms, body, and, more deceptively effective, the hip joints of Ali. Now in the eleventh Ali stopped in a corner, repeatedly helped out by Mercante, who broke up the fighters time and again (and once put his finger in Frazier's eye). Not giving and receiving, but purely receiving, Ali played a dangerous game with the Frazier hook. Finally, the inevitable happened. The hook landed hard on the chin. Ali wobbled. I looked at poor Angelo standing straight up from his corner crouch as if he himself had received the blow, yelling to clinch, move, move, move. Ali tried to move on legs that would not respond. I looked at the clock: two minutes to go. *God, he'll never weather this.* I glanced at Budd who looked as stricken as Jack Kent Cooke. But it is difficult to go to an Ali fight without some surprises. Ali, defying age, layoff rust, and diminished reflexes, showed why he was regarded by a generation as a superhuman. Reeling, rubber-legged, bouncing off ring ropes, sitting on the middle strand, he absorbed a brutal, bestial beating by another superb athlete with a lion's heart. In the end he staggered unsteadily to his corner to be met by a tearful Bundini and a grimly purposeful Angelo Dundee and Sarria. Stoner sat down in amazement. We all had virtually collapsed in relief at the bell. Angelo said he didn't need anything medical, so I went back to the corner coaching with Budd yelling at Ali.

5. *Twelfth, thirteenth, fourteenth:* Frazier chased and

pounded but Ali kept even with his beautiful combinations and straight right hands. Frazier was still grinning, but it was a lopsided grin, his face contorted by abrasions, hematomas, and contusions. Saliva drooled from his swollen lips and he was breathing in gasps. Ali was still boxing coolly. You have to admire Ali's cool. His postures are classic, a duplication of the Dying Gaul statues. I felt that the fourteenth round was crucial, and Ali won that big. Joe was arm-weary, tired, and virtually punched out. Ali was exhausted, but summoning unthought-of reserved energy for the final assault. The fifteenth would tell the tale. A perfect fight, down to the wire.

6. *Fifteenth:* I turned to Budd and said we need this round to win by a narrow margin, and saw a left hook coming from the Battery and landing with smashing authority on Ali's face as he withdrew his head in the time-honored style that has kept him champion for a decade. Ali saw it too, but seemed powerless to extract another inch from his already extended position and crashed to the canvas. Almost immediately he arose (at the count of three) and received the mandatory eight count. During that instant your mind does fantastic tricks. Time dissolves. Frozen faces, as you alternately look at the fighter and the crowd. Slow motion replaying of the knockdown. Pleading in your mind for him to get up. Hopes for a miracle, a lucky punch on a wide-open Frazier, careless with the scent of the kill in his nose. Horror on the face of Dundee, and disgust, too. Tears streaming down Bundini's face. You look into the crowd, spot your wife and the Dundee family, wife and children, mouths agape, tears in their eyes, and then into the hard faces of the crowd that came to see just this, and see disbelief. Oh, no, it couldn't happen to *him*. He makes time stand still. *He* comes back. He is

your youth gone, never to return, and yet, look, your young kid isn't young any more, he is a 29-year-old fighter. Survival is his main problem right now. Not winning, he has blown that, but survival. Then someone says, "Look at Ali, I think his jaw is busted," and he *is* holding it strangely, bloody saliva drooling on his chest, exhaustion in his eyes as he chases his quarry. Then a hard look at Ali's vacant stare and down at his jaw. What has been a small lemon-sized knot is suddenly a large orange-sized lump, but he is fighting. Those who doubted the man's heart and stamina must now swallow hard. The man has no dog in him. Neither has Frazier. This is the most that one can ask of this rude, brutal game of boxing: an even contest between equally matched fighters of the same caliber. And this we have seen on this night. Two champions, of different styles, from different worlds, but of the same fighting heart. The crowd is now on its feet, even the most callous fan, the coolest customer, has his heart on his sleeve and is yelling. The final bell comes at a clinch and both men are too exhausted to break momentarily but wink at each other and fall into the arms of their cornermen. Who won? It is fair to say that the majority of the people there do not know how this will be scored. A buzz fills the Garden and the ring fills with people.

Ali is exhausted but pushes away all help from Angie and Bundini. I examine his jaw. It is hard to tell if it is broken. I must exit to arrange for X-rays to be taken. The scorecards are in and are being read. Two officials have it extremely close for Frazier, one has it 11–4 for Frazier. A psychiatric consultation is being sought for him. Frazier is too tired to have his arm raised, he passes us in a swirl of attendants, his feet barely touching the ground. Ali tries to smile at him, and we are swept away by the crowds. I leave the ring and look for

Angelo Dundee and a young Ali watch a thoroughbred work out at a race track following roadwork. "Even horses do roadwork."
[HOWARD BINGHAM]

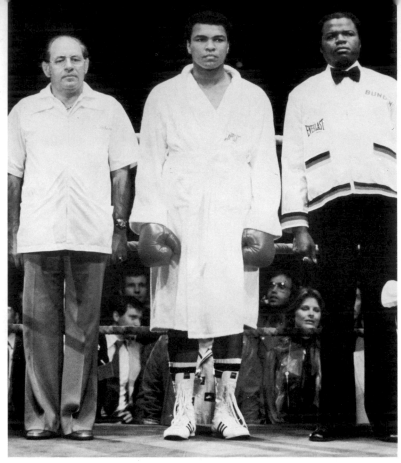

Ali, Bundini and I stand for "The Star Spangled Banner" in Munich. Classy press person is Candice Bergen. [HOWARD BINGHAM]

The two men responsible for my involvement in boxing, Manager Angelo Dundee, Promoter Chris Dundee.

Luis Sarria, silent, watchful, powerful, all-knowing Cuban trainer. [HOWARD BINGHAM]

Brother Rahaman and ever-present bodyguard Pat Patterson (in background) at press conference.
[GERALDINE SCHULBERG]

Photographer Howard Bingham, Ali's loyal friend, meets Ali for Central Park roadwork. [LUISITA PACHECO]

My son Ferdie in the arms of the gentle bear, Heavyweight Champion Sonny Liston. [PAUL'S STUDIO]

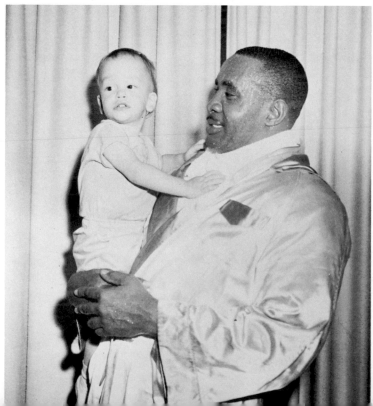

Ali, with a look of real interest, listening to Howard Cosell, with a look of
real hair. [HOWARD BINGHAM]

The ventriloquist act. A doctor dummy on the lap of the Heavyweight Champion. [LUISITA PACHECO]

True love in the dressing room: Bundini hugs Angelo as I sew up Ali after the Foster fight. [HOWARD BINGHAM]

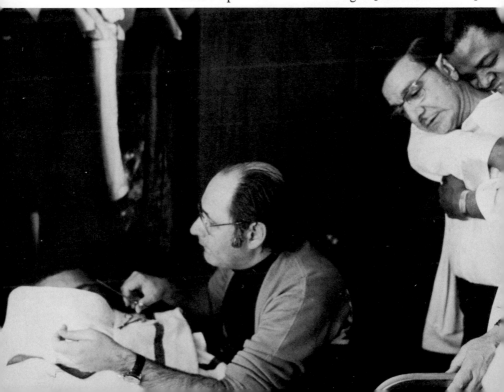

Ali and Marciano trade jabs for computer fight. [MURRAY WORONER]

An out-of-shape Ali meets an in-shape Marciano as producer-writer-innovator Murray Woroner looks on.

Writer-mentor-friend Budd Schulberg—the man who refined the art of boxing authorship. [LUISITA PACHECO]

Norman Lear: two writers compare notes before Norton-Ali fight. [LUISITA PACHECO]

Joe Louis, who brought dignity to boxing and pride to a people . . . my personal hero. [LUISITA PACHECO]

Boxing makes one travel in a rarefied atmosphere; it transcends social strata. Luisita and I meet HRH The Prince of Wales; a jubilant Mickey Duff looks on.

Sarria speaks through his knowing hands. [HOWARD BINGHAM]

Ali launches into a benediction of John Francis Xavier Condon, Angel of Madison Square Garden publicity, as Bundini haggles for extra tickets with Harry Markson. [HOWARD BINGHAM]

Joe Frazier fought Ali three times . . . wars of attrition paralleled only by Veraun. [AP WIREPHOTO]

Once was enough for George Foreman.

But for Ken Norton three is not enough. [LUISITA PACHECO]

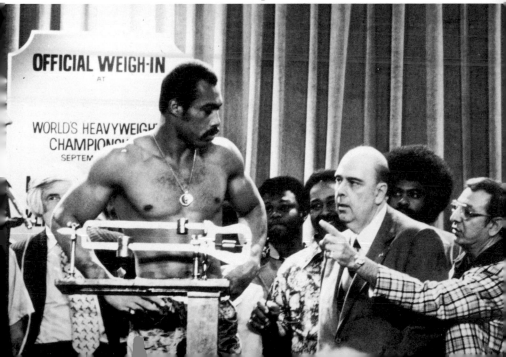

John Marshall, producer, Herbert Muhammad, shrewd manipulator of Ali's fortunes, Angelo Dundee and Elizabeth Marshall on movie set of *The Greatest*. [LUISITA PACHECO]

Marshall's masterpiece of cinema casting: notice how much the real-life Angelo looks like the real Ernest Borgnine. A full-maned, silver-haired John Marley was unmistakably me. [CRICKET CLUB]

"Dammit, Drew, give back the bathrobe." [LUISITA PACHECO]

my New York doctor to arrange for hospitalization for Ali, and fortunately I have a great plastic surgeon with me, Dr. Howard Gordon from Miami. We are swept into the dressing room. Police are punching people outside who are trying to force their way inside. The general mood is bleak.

Always in step, understanding without speaking, my friend and I.
[LUISITA PACHECO]

9·The Broken Jaw and Ken Norton

MARCH 1973

The ankle injury happened a week before the fight, and although it kept Ali from running, it did not put a halt to his daily training routine. He was attended by the San Diego Chargers' doctor who, it is presumed, is all-knowing in the matter of ankle injuries. Trainers taped the ankle before the fight, which may or may not have been the thing to do. Personally, from my examination, his ankle was in good shape by fight time, and not a factor in the fight at all. His hand injury also falls into this category in that Ali has always had knuckle injuries, which he has aggravated by his nonstop series of fights over the past two years. He did not give things time to heal properly; however, I must say that most fighters I have attended (and that runs into hundreds over the past thirteen years of taking care of all of Angie's fighters and all of Chris' visiting fighters in Miami Beach) had this type of hand injury, and it can be considered part of the fighters' plight to have continually sore hands. It does not impede their punching if properly treated.

Ali took Ken Norton cheaply, and off Norton's performance his opinion was probably justified. I feel Jimmy Ellis could have disposed of Norton in less than five, and a healthy Ali could have dropped him almost as the whim took him. Ken's condition for the fight was excellent, while Ali was bad, mentally and physically. Norton had a hypnotist, which we neutralized with Evil Eye Finkle and, as a saver, Jimmy Grippo.

The broken jaw occurred in the second round without a doubt, in my mind, although Ali showed slight bleeding from the mouth in the first, which led Angie to assume it might have been then. My observation comes from the fact that Ali exclaimed, "I think my jaw is broken! I heard something pop!" and my physical exam at that moment between the second and third rounds. The exam revealed a jaw fractured, but in line. The separation is palpated (felt with the fingertip) as well as a peculiar sound evoked (crepitation), which feels and sounds like finely crunched glass. The key to stopping the fight then is whether the injury is life threatening, or whether the fighter is in danger of permanent disability. Neither was the case at the end of the second round. I did not tell Ali then that it was broken, but spoke of a cracked tooth. The reason is that the responsibility lies with the chief second, in this case Angelo Dundee, and I wanted him to have time between rounds to discuss it.

By the end of the next round, the third, Angelo had been apprised of the lesion and, in a hurried conference, we decided to tell the fighter and see if he could put Norton away and have done with the fight. He was told and he refused to let us stop it. Here I must interject that if either of the afore-mentioned criteria were met—had Ali's life or future abilities been at stake—I would have stopped it by signaling the commission doctor (who later told me he thanked God we did not call him, since the overflow crowd would have really been aroused by the fight being stopped at the second or third, after paying one hundred smackers, regardless of what the fighter wanted). You may think the fight should have been stopped, regardless of what the crowd wanted, but decisions of this type are made with many considerations in mind when it comes to Ali. He was about to sign the Frazier fight for the upcoming summer, and a lucrative Foreman fight to follow. He was not in pain (and did not mention pain once in the whole fight) and he, as well as we, thought he could handle Norton easily. It did not turn out that way, again for many reasons, but mainly for the ones we have mentioned: poor conditioning, poor mental attitude, nagging small injuries, and, of course, the broken jaw. What would he have done had he been in his super condition (as in the Frazier fight) even with a broken jaw? Knock Norton out before the fifth, I think. Everything caught up with Ali in San Diego that afternoon. However, it's obvious in retrospect that the press was premature in dismissing him as washed up after this dismal performance. They confused cause and effect. He had a broken jaw which caused him to fight a lousy fight. But, really, was it a lousy fight if we know that he fought with it broken since the second? When looked at with a cold, dispassionate eye, I think we can admire that example of ring bravery, much as Basilio was praised for his one-eyed fight with Robinson. The fight business is tough and although everyone always conceded that Basilio was one tough cookie, no one up to that point really comprehended that Pretty Ali had that kind of grit in him. And again he surprised everyone, including me, with his show of valor and determination. Wouldn't it have been easier to quit? There is no disgrace in a fight stopped with a broken jaw.

The postfight dressing-room scene was grossly and incorrectly described by a wire guy who was nowhere in sight. Only one man from the press was in the room: Brady from Washington. One photographer at the last minute admitted— the *Sports Illustrated* guy. The reason was that in the midst of all that hysteria I needed to introduce some quiet for some clear thinking. The commission doctor, Dr. Lundeen, was helpful in lining up Dr. Lancaster, the plastic surgeon, and the hospital. I got the limo ready and put Ali, Lundeen, and a Muslim bodyguard, as well as Gene Kilroy, into it; then we went off to the hospital without the usual comet tail of followers. Angelo was left to handle the press, and another section handled Ali's wife who was hysterical and needed a lot of attention to get her admitted to the hospital. The operation was blissfully quiet, and Dr. Lancaster did masterful work. He has a great deal of experience, having been stuck in a Vietnam hospital doing nothing but maxilofacial surgery for a year. Dr. Lundeen assisted and both did beautifully in handling a difficult patient, and the hospital did a great job on security, although the usual share of hangers-on managed to slip through to the recovery room and wake up Ali to ask him the usual *"You OK, man?"*

The next morning we had an unusual conference with a pensive Ali and Angelo, Herbert Muhammad, and me. The fact was that Ali had strayed away from his religion and its beliefs for some time. Now I pointed out to Ali that it had cost him, since he could fool all people but he could not fool the Lord. Ali digested that and all other criticisms manfully, and Herbert remarked that it took a white man to set him straight. My feeling is that his religion is what sustains Ali, emotionally and physically, and whether you agree or not with the Muslims, you have to admit that its rules of physical well-being must have been written by Whitey Bimstein, the greatest trainer who ever worked in a corner, for they are exactly what a boxer, or any athlete, should live by.

I felt that Ali, in proper condition and without the constant energy-sapping action of the past two years, would have a chance to defeat Foreman if they fought within the ensuing twelve months. I could not see him losing to anyone else. It remained to be seen whether, having tasted the high life, he would return to the monastic ways of his religion. He was currently suspended so that did not help him in abiding by his faith. However, Herbert, being the son of Elijah, had a great deal of power over him, and Herbert is a good man, interested in Ali's well-being, a sensible man who could rein in Ali's high life and return him to becoming the super athlete that he still was.

10·The Rumble in the Jungle— George Foreman

OCTOBER 1974

Bud Collins of the *Boston Globe* was the pleasantest of companions as we traveled together on Air France to Zaire, but Bud was all that was good about that trip. It involved six stops and lasted twenty-six hours and our luggage was lost. We did get to Africa in the end, but I for one am never going to do it again for fun. We weren't the only ones.

Over one hundred American newsmen knew that there was something amiss when their direct charter plane to Zaire landed in Iceland. A modest knowledge of geography would suffice to indicate that this was not the shortest route to Kinshasa. After many weary hours of jet travel they found themselves in Luxembourg and heard the astounding news that the heavyweight champion, George Foreman, who had taken the crown off Joe Frazier's battered brow in two rounds in January 1973, was cut, and the Great Fight was in doubt. That was enough for most veteran newsmen, and most followed Jim Murray and Shirley Povich to the nearest terminal counter to begin renegotiating their return to the States and sanity. Theirs was a triumph of experience over optimism.

Reggie Gutteridge, Britain's answer to Howard Cosell,

figured he was in for a bad day when he arrived in Zaire and strapped on his artificial leg backward. But he gave the Zaire porters and police an even nastier shock when they saw a small disheveled Englishman walking toward them with one foot pointed in the opposite direction.

Bud and I were leaving stop number five for Zaire when I heard the shocking news and decided to press on to see if I could be of help, and to hang around for the fight if it was not delayed too long. The prospect of seeing Foreman face Ali for the real championship of the world was too much to let go for lack of trying. Ali had revenged himself on Ken Norton, winning a tough twelve-round decision over him in September 1973, and four months later had turned the tables on Joe Frazier in similar fashion. So we had the official champion, Foreman, up against our man, Ali, who still was the champion in our book, no matter what the official commission had declared. This fight would settle things, and I wasn't going to miss it.

Zaire has a small airport but a large army, and on arriving I had the feeling that I had landed in the Havana airport in the midst of the Castro takeover. Zaire customs officials have a brusque no-nonsense approach to foreigners. No attempt is made to speak English, although most do speak English and their French is a patois that even a Haitian wouldn't understand. Because of the fight, the government had issued orders for a general softening of their normal attitude, and several actually tried to smile, unused muscles creaking with the strain. It all had the aspect of Parents' Day at Dachau. Fortunately I had foreseen this, and wore my bright green Muhammad Ali jacket with his name emblazoned on the pocket.

A small man in an official interpreters' Mao jacket bowed low, solved all problems, and I was whisked past a long line of travelers and into a small Volkswagen bus. We left the brightly illuminated airport and shot into the darkness of the highway toward a string of lights in the far distance which marked the president's VIP compound, known as N'Seli.

N'Seli is one hour out of Kinshasa, or roughly forty miles. And I mean roughly. Rumor has it that it was designed and built by the Red Chinese in the period when they were trying to influence this emerging African nation. The official version is that it was built solely by Africans, but the impression one gets favors the rumor, especially when you see all signs written in Chinese and French, and the first building you encounter is a huge elaborately built and lit oriental pagoda. Anchored in front of the villas, riding the mile-wide tide of the Zaire River is the president's yacht, named the *President Mobutu,* oddly enough, and illuminated by spotlights. Another rumor has it that the Chinese raised the U.S.S. *Panay,* rebuilt it, and presented it to President Mobutu. I should know, I started the rumor.

Once inside the sumptuous villa I heard the unmistakable rumble of Ali's voice in the midst of a vituperative tirade aimed at Larry Merchant, the *Post's* sportswriter, for asking a provocative racial question. So starved for company and medical care was the group that they all welcomed me effusively. The whole group lined up for shots for various real and imagined afflictions. I brought twenty-four disposable syringes and used them all in the first twenty-four hours. Coretta Clay, Ali's aunt and *chef de cuisine,* then served up a wonderful dish of chicken and soul-sauced cabbage. It was the first and absolutely the last edible meal I had while in Zaire.

Muhammad Ali was in wonderful shape physically, but I could see he did not enjoy his usual optimistic spirits. He felt, quite correctly I think, that if he left Zaire while Foreman's wound was healing, he would not be able to prevent Foreman from following suit, and once out of the country

Foreman would not return, while the title shot and five million dollars would vanish. Maybe never to reappear. I know one thing, Ali was ready, maybe readier than at any time since the first Liston fight. He was in perfect shape, and his mind was razor sharp. He had what fight people call a "fine edge." Foreman, by contrast, was physically sluggish and mentally apathetic. He was going to lose his crown. I am not saying that the cut was inflicted on purpose; this would be absurd. I am saying he was lucky to get a six-week reprieve. Meantime Ali was wondering what the international laws were concerning detaining American citizens in a foreign country over six weeks.

The cut was inflicted by an experienced sparring partner, who was covering up his face with his elbows and inadvertently sliced open the brow of the champion. The cut was under his right eyebrow, along the ridge of bone that forms the eye socket. It was jagged, not smooth, and deep. President Mobutu's two physicians were called, as was Foreman's own physician. They all urged suturing, which was the only way to close that type of wound tightly and have a chance at repair in the six weeks that the fight date had been set back. Dick Sadler concurred, but the champion demurred. The Heavyweight Champion of the World does not like needles of any kind, and his word is law in that camp. Therefore, his cut was taped shut with butterflies, small pieces of tape with small niches cut out of the side, placed over a wound. Ideally they are used when a cut is smooth and superficial. Here the wound was jagged and deep. The implications are obvious to any physician, as they are to any boxing person. That cut will reopen—either in training or in the fight.

Naturally, a press conference was called, and first Foreman, then Ali appeared to reassure all and sundry that both would stay in Zaire until the rescheduled October 30 date for the fight. Foreman had been sort of a recluse, partly because of his nature, and also because the Zaire government did not like the idea of his walking around with a huge German police dog. It seems that to the Zairians a police dog is symbolic of the tough century of Belgian rule. Belgian police controlled crowds with vicious police dogs—and upon their departure the Zairians fell on the dogs and killed them and ate them. Apparently, the sight of one of these huge dogs now fills them with either dread or hunger.

Anyhow, Foreman's idea of reassurance was to give the press a rambling quote wherein he stated that he loved the country and would stay until he left. It wasn't very clear to begin with, and it must have lost something in translation.

Ali was in his usual rare form when given a platform. First he stepped into the ring, stripped to his waist, smooth butter-brown skin glistening in the African heat, not a ripple of fat visible. At a low 215 pounds he shadowboxed for a round, then noticed a large placard on the ropes, facing the audience with its back to him. Most fighters don't like anything on or in their ring. Ali picked it up in disgust to fling it out, but the shock on the audience's face told him to look at it, and when he did his jaw dropped to the canvas: he was gingerly holding a portrait of President Mobutu. Swiftly, gently, he replaced it and resumed his flicking, flitting, dancing to a roar of approval from the assembled natives. He stopped in midring and led first one side, then the other, in an African war chant devised by the natives for this fight:

"Ali boom a lay, Ali boom a lay, Ali boom a lay!"

Obviously in his best form, Ali continued until time for the press conference. The chant kept up as he sat down: *"Ali kill him, Ali kill him!"*

He then swore to stay in Africa until the fight took place, stated it openly and strongly, satisfied everyone in sight, kissed a few babies, signed autographs, and sauntered back to his compound past the ever present assembled guards. (I loved observing the militant guards and sketched them every time I could, although I had to give them the sketches when

I finished. The pose I loved and kept was the one wherein a couple on guard would be holding their guns with one hand, and holding hands with the other.) At any rate the crisis was temporarily over, both fighters swearing to stay and have it out in six weeks. Both went to their respective villas, and Don King and Tshimpumpu Wa Tshimpumpu went to church to give thanks—one that his finances were spared, the other that his life was spared.

The weeks prior to fight week had just about seen the sinking of the Don King flagship on the troubled promotional waters of the fight game. First, his promised avalanche of tourists had not materialized. And a fortunate thing it was, too, since it turned out to be the ripoff of the decade. Monies were paid in the States, but no one in Kinshasa got the message so that the promised and paid-for hotel rooms were not available, and the rest of the goodies were not to be had. Lawsuits were flying. Next, a poster idea went down like a Belgian hot dog, the slogan being senseless and offensive to the native Africans: FROM SLAVESHIP TO CHAMPIONSHIP. Huge posters were printed bearing this headline. Africans stared uncomprehendingly at the slogan. After all, Africans are the ones who stayed and *sent* the slaves: they were the slave traders, not the slaves, and they could not relate to the message in the sense that American blacks can relate. So that fizzled out. King also had envisioned a joyful return to the source of basic American black music, which some say is the only true original black music, by having a three-day jazz festival. Unfortunately the simple rhythms of the Congo still persist in their original form (especially on Air Zaire), and the natives have not become sophisticated enough to dig the furthest extension of their rhythms as encompassed by the Pointer Sisters and James Brown. So the three-day festival was a huge bust, artistically and financially, and both the artists and the audience were left with a confused and unsatisfied feeling. The hotel was left with an unsatisfied feeling that the one-hundred-fifty-thousand-dollar room service tab incurred by the hungry musicians was not going to be paid. The Zaire government acted quickly, shut down Air Zaire reservations, and stranded the musicians in their hotels until the tab *was* paid. As the United States government was getting ready to send a gunboat down the Zaire River, the Zaire government recanted and decided to let the musicians go, but kept their sound equipment hostage. If you follow modern music, you are aware that this is like letting a man go, but keeping his heart and circulatory system. King struck another deal with the Liberian government, which was bank-rolling the abortive music festival, and they finally bailed out the instruments. But add another thirty gray hairs to King's electrified mane.

As it turned out, the more than a month's delay was heaven-sent for the promotion. In that time the stadium was finished, the tickets were printed in Philadelphia (they had been returned because someone in Philadelphia had misspelled President Mobutu's name), the parking and sanitary facilities were completed, the satellite connections had been made, and the roof that was to keep the monsoon rains off the fighters was constructed. Foreman had spent the time getting into shape, and his eye cut was revealed not to be very serious. Ali had come down a bit from his physical peak, but still maintained his great shape, and his desire to get the title back was as keen as ever.

The night of the fight arrived, and the team began to gather. Luis Sarria had come close to losing his foot as the result of a gangrenous infection which had been poorly treated in my absence, and now, in Angelo's villa, he quietly shuffled to his room and packed his gear. Every once in a while he painfully made his way to the TV set to continue his watch of President Mobutu's face floating through the clouds. Bud Collins' and my luggage had never arrived, and Angelo loaned the now pungent Bud a shirt while I took a Cuban Gualyabera shirt from Budd Schulberg to work the fight.

I tried to sleep between eleven and three in order to be fresh for our four A.M. starting date, but was constantly being interrupted by camp people seeking last-minute cures for varied ailments. C. B. Atkins entered to talk of Ali's hands. Prior to this fight I had always fixed his hands so that he could punch with impunity and felt that it was wise to do so this time, but Ali and his manager now felt that this contributed to his getting tired. Finally we arrived at a crazy compromise that we only deaden his left hand, since he would use that more often, but I felt that his strong opinion would negate this compromise. Frankly, since he had decided to listen to reason and had actually quit using the heavy bag in training, his hands were greatly improved and did not require stringent measures. As it turned out, we left his hands alone.

Angelo quietly packed his bag, exuding an air of quiet confidence. Outside by the buses the camp followers gathered, mostly wearing worried looks. Ali and his family and in-laws appeared in a restrained mood, but when the buses and cars began to roll an air of joviality pervaded the bus. The talk was light and Belinda, looking truly beautiful in an original African gown, was making the passengers laugh with her banter. Belinda is a tall, graceful, handsome woman with a flashing, disarming smile and friendly manner. I am always at a loss in how to treat her since she is a Muslim woman and not supposed to associate too closely with white people; however, it seems to bother me more than her, since she is warm and friendly whenever we meet. The night was quiet as we drove through the jungle to the stadium, and it was hard to reconcile our surroundings with the reason for our being there.

Soon we came to the outskirts of the area where the

stadium was located. Although it was quite a distance from Kinshasa, the street crowd was huge. As people recognized Ali's convoy, "Ali boom a lay" was heard from every up-turned face. Ali beamed. These were his people and his crowd. He knew he had them all on his side, and we were able to enter peacefully with practically none of the shoving and pushing that usually accompanies the arrival of a champion in New York, Rome, or any of the other "civilized" cities where fights are held.

The dressing room was carpeted in blue, freshly painted, and very clean. We all set about preparing ourselves for the fight. Ali was exuberant. I went to take a look at the ring and stadium, and was happy to see every seat taken by orderly, well-behaved people. A regiment of native dancers, with feathers and beads flying, were entertaining the crowd, and they truly added a wonderful dimension to the night.

The afternoon of the fight Angelo, as is his custom, had gone to the stadium to check the ring, and found it sadly wanting. The ring canvas was loose and not properly padded, and the ropes were sagging horribly. It took Angelo almost two hours to put things right, and only then did he return to the compound, satisfied that the fight would go on under the best possible circumstances. In the light of later accusations that Angelo loosened the ropes during the fight, it seems ironic that the fight took place under good conditions because of the professional thoroughness of this top pro.

The champion and his trainers had acted like bush leaguers throughout the training period, and continued to maintain a truculent attitude during the preparation period. For example, before fighters' hands are taped, one of the opposing cornermen usually travels to the dressing room of the other fighter, and watches his hands being wrapped.

Angelo sent me to ask what time they wanted to wrap. Sadler answered that nine-thirty would be fine, and since it was already nine-twenty-five, I took their man, Doc, and

135

walked him to our dressing room in order to admit him through the paratroop guards. That being accomplished, I walked back through the stadium to the Foreman dressing room. There I was held up at the door by the troops. Along with me was an African interpreter, who was also shut out. I began calling for Sadler. Silence. Presently the door cracked open to admit the African, but not me. I put my foot in the door and a scuffle ensued, during which I heard Sadler tell the African to tell the troops to give me the bum's rush. Since I understood enough French to know when to retreat, I was saved the embarrassment of being thrown out bodily, but it was nonetheless bush. It seemed to exemplify the entourage's attitude through the whole Foreman championship tenure. Steaming, I walked over to our dressing room and threw Doc out, and he, at least, seemed embarrassed by the way things were being done in the champ's dressing room.

We walked back together and I was admitted with a mumbled half lie–apology by Sadler. "Gee, Doc, I didn't know you were out there, we weren't quite ready."

Foreman was lying quietly under a mountain of towels. I thought of the contrast in Ali's dressing room, where hyperactivity is the norm, and everything but animal acts are walking in and out and performing, and Ali is usually clowning and moving, moving, moving.

The wrapping was done in a grim quiet. Archie Moore was holding his mysterious bag with its unknown contents. His publicity sense was not diminished by years of retirement. He was very serious. I represented the enemy, and had to be treated as such. This was *war*. I have been in thousands of opposing dressing rooms and the fraternity of cornermen usually treat each other lightly. After all, they will see each other again and again over the years, another thousand times, so what is the point of this childlike posturing and menacing attitude among professionals? Even the boxers are friendly.

Pugilism is, after all, a sports event, not World War III. Foreman seemed concerned and too quiet. He was not warmed up and soon the opening bell would sound.

I returned to our show biz atmosphere in time to hear the usual rumble between Ali and Bundini. Bundini gets some turkey to make Ali a new robe and trunks before every fight, which Bundini either turns over for a fast profit or keeps for historical purposes (will he start an Ali museum in Harrisburg after he retires?). Ali, as the mood takes him, either indulges him or brings his own robe, usually a gift from his hosts or a fellow performer (Elvis Presley gave him a beautiful gem-encrusted robe in Las Vegas which Ali particularly admired, since it had emblazoned on his back PEOPLE'S CHAMPION). This time some Africans had made him a native robe which looked very African, yet met the decorum of the prize ring. Ali loved it and declined Bundini's robe, which set Bundini off and earned him his usual once-a-fight slap from Ali.

Now it was quiet in the dressing room, only the cornermen ready to go, and Herbert walked in with a message from his father, the leader of the Black Muslim religion, the honorable Elijah Muhammad. Ali and Herbert went into the shower area, and Herbert read the lengthy but inspirational message to Ali whose eyes clouded in a rare show of emotion. The fight became a religious experience from that point on, and it took on the aspects of the Crusades as we formed up to walk into the arena.

Angelo and I took up the front position and Ali followed with Youngblood and Bundini at his side, followed by Sarria dragging his bloody feet forward painfully. Then came Kilroy who had done so much to make my stay comfortable, lending me clothes, arguing with air-line personnel, feeding me from his privately hoarded stock of food, and generally being very good company. C. B. Atkins, Durham, and the rest of the camp followed. Up on the ring apron bodyguard Pat Patterson was holding the ropes for Ali. At ringside Herbert and his party was seated, looking a little worried but composed.

As we entered the arena a loud roar swelled up from the assemblage. I've heard crowds respond to Ali throughout the world, and I thought I would never feel the electricity of the first Frazier fight again, but here, in the middle of the morning in Africa, I felt a completely unique surge of love and excitement come pouring over the ring. People were chanting the Ali chant and singing, laughing, and some crying.

In what was another bush move, Foreman let us stand in midring for another ten minutes before appearing, which, if calculated to annoy Ali, had exactly the opposite effect, since Ali is, if nothing else, a consummate showman, and does not mind hogging the spotlight for ten uninterrupted minutes. The cheering went on for that length of time and then the lion's roar as Foreman ran out in a trot, followed by the chunky Sadler and the two former great champions, Sandy Saddler and Archie Moore, the latter clutching his mysterious bag, followed by the ever present sparring partner with the bullhorn. He had spent the weeks before the fight milling around the lobby of the hotel screaming into the bullhorn. *"Oh yeah, oh yeah. . . . Ali in three."* Now he took his place behind our corner with his bullhorn ready to disturb Ali's concentration. A tough Muslim gave him a curt suggestion he could not refuse, and we never heard him again.

After an emotional moment when the Anthem was played, we moved to midring for the instructions. Zack Clayton, a black referee of enormous talent and experience, warned both fighters, and moved back to start the fight. Ali turned in a silent prayer and looked down at Herbert's worried face. They were clearly locked in a silent communication. Herbert prayed and one could sense the love between these two separate but similar men.

Now the bell and the roar of anticipation. Ali, slipping and punching lightly, won the first round. Foreman did what Angelo had predicted. In fact, Angelo had perfectly predicted all of Foreman's moves, and pointed out his flaws. He had said that Foreman blocks punches with his hands held high in front of his body, a sucker for feints and body shots, and sure to get arm-weary soon. His punches are wide, with arm strength fading with each punch. His head never moves, a stationary target for a sharp puncher like Ali. This meant Ali could afford to put strength behind each punch and not go tentatively looking for a bobbing head like Frazier's; Joe is hard to hit with solid punches early in a fight.

Foreman moved full of confidence like a hunter, used to a bit of running after his prey before the final kill. He didn't mind losing the first round. After all, how long could an aging Ali run on his toes like that, and his punches, though sharp, had no sting in them.

The second round opened with a sharp surprise for all the millions watching, but especially to us. Ali stopped dead in his tracks and leaned on the ropes. This is what Foreman wanted to happen after a few rounds of dancing and body shots, but he seemed perplexed and hesitant to take what Ali was offering. He began a ponderous attack to Ali's flanks. Ali was leaning on the ropes with both arms tucked in to his sides, gloves held up to the side of his face, and leaning back out of reach of any head shots that came his way. It is time to explain that Ali's system works for him because of his tremendous reflexes and because of his size. Ali is tall at six foot three and leaning back he is almost impossible to reach. He has a glove radar inbuilt that permits him to sense the upcoming punch and adjust accordingly. Punches were flying but Ali was not getting hit, as films will show, if studied carefully. Films are nice afterward, but during the fight it wrecks a strong man's nervous system to see your guy's body being pummeled by the strongest puncher in the fight game. Now Foreman is warming to the task; he is bracing himself, and you can feel his toes digging into the canvas as he lets fly with his thunderous punches like Big Bertha in World War I.

In our huddled corner I feel like a small child watching his father being pummeled by the neighborhood thug. Bundini is halfway up the ring stairs, I have him by the seat of the pants to keep him from getting too excited and costing us the fight, and I am yelling also. On the ring apron Angelo is pounding his fist, yelling, and behind him Youngblood and Kilroy, all screaming the same thing:

"Get off the ropes . . . get off the ropes."

Even the stoical Cuban Sarria is out of control, yelling in Spanish, *"Fuera . . . Fuera de la soga . . . Ali . . . Ali . . . fuera."*

Finally the bell rang, and we all rushed to help in the corner. Our corner is usually quiet and very professionally efficient, run as it is by the top cornerman in the world, Angelo Dundee; however, nervous anxiety has overcome us and we all yell as one, "What in the hell are you doing on the ropes? Stay off the ropes. . . . That is how you blew the Frazier fight. . . . What is the matter with you?"

Ali looks annoyed, which is rare for him, since he is the Mr. Cool of the fight game. "Shut up! All of you. I know what I am doing. Don't tell me nothing. I don't want to hear another word. Shut up." He stares us down, then his compassionate side takes over. He cannot stay mad for longer than a split second. He explains, "The chump has nothing. He has nothing. He can't hurt me. He can't hit me. I'm going to let this sucker punch himself out."

Now that the plan has taken shape in Ali's head, he sets about implementing it. He continues to back into the ropes all through the third round. Foreman is wearing down like a windup toy. He looks annoyed, then flustered and frustrated. The fourth round starts and Ali is cooking with the verbal darts and psychological ploys. At one point a devastating right hand thumps into his flank. Ali grins and says to Foreman, "That was good, George, but it doesn't hurt. Try it again. Here it is open, George. Take another shot, chump."

Foreman found himself listening and trying to figure this out. *Should I try it again? Is it a sucker shot to counter? No, I'll try a left . . . but maybe that is what he thinks I'll think.*

And so it goes through the fourth with Ali outthinking Foreman and Foreman mentally and physically running down. Ali is not getting hit solid shots where it hurts, but he is beginning to pepper Foreman's face with solid jabs. The champ is reddening and lumping up and to our amazement his legs are getting all tangled up, a sure sign that the gas is dangerously low in his tank. *Any time now,* I think, and look at Angelo. I can see a smile now through the frown. I yell over to Herbert "He is ours now" at the end of the fourth round, and even the writers are nodding at me as if to agree. Ali looks over at David Frost and Jim Brown and winks. Frost is elated, being a big Ali fan, but Brown is having trouble managing a smile since it is known he has a heavy bet on Foreman.

Now Ali is into his thing: he is leading the crowds in their Ali yell, he is mugging for the press, he is looking over at George's corner and making faces, and talking, talking, talking in George's face. Foreman is a beaten fighter as the fifth starts. He buckles and staggers through the round. His punches have no steam, his eyes are glazed pools of exhaustion. His corner is helpless to devise a better plan. They cannot help him. No one can help him. There in the midst of a black nation, a black man is about to lose his world title to perhaps the ultimate black man before a black audience presided over by a black referee and for a black promoter, in the midst of a black African night. Foreman seems to sense the futility of his struggle but is incapable of changing his battle plan. No one has ever stood up before to the Foreman battering ram.

The seventh is merely a prelude to the end. Now we are all exhorting in the corner, "Don't take a chance, Ali, put him away, he is yours, take him." Ali nods like a matador being told by his *cuadrilla* to go for the kill.

The eighth opens with a mild attack by a weary Foreman. He is doing better but is foolishly unaware of Ali's punching power. Suddenly Ali begins to punch with authority. Sharp hard jabs, hooks, right crosses. All thud with precision into Foreman's swelling face, then suddenly, as the round is about to end, Ali begins a five-punch combination which, as seen on films, is a thing of improvised beauty. Foreman flays the air with his huge arm, spins around Ali whose glove is cocked to throw the final shot, but as he sees Foreman in that last fall he holds his punch, and Foreman does a perfect jackknife onto the canvas, rolls over, and seems to have found a home, relieved that his ordeal is at an end.

Zack bends over, counting precisely with the timekeeper. George attempts to get up but does not beat the count. It is academic whether he will or not, for if he gets up, Ali is waiting with the fire in his eye that portends mayhem. George is well advised by his senses to stay down. His corner is also ambivalent. They seem relieved that no further harm will come to their man. Ali is not by nature a killer and he, as well as we, are relieved, but most of all we are exuberant. The world heavyweight championship belongs to Ali again after a ten-year period. Unheard of! Now joy breaks loose. Gene Kilroy is the first to jump into the ring. The rest of us tumble in. Panic. Crying, laughing, pushing, shoving, and all the usual after the fight, only more so. I lose my glasses in midring and chance losing my life diving after them, but the prospect of twenty-six hours on a plane without being able to read is worth that risk.

Our convoy lined up and we inched our way through the thousands of fans who had stayed to get a glimpse of Ali. Then we were rolling along the open countryside, where hundreds of natives lined the sides of the road. Arms upraised, they chanted Ali, Ali, Ali, Ali and held up small children to see him. Budd Schulberg, George Plimpton, and I sat in the back of a bus, smiling wanly and comparing the scene to the liberation of Paris. We who had shared the second coming of Ali in that glorious night of black awakening in Atlanta, and shared the bitter hospital scene after the first Frazier fight, and the tough night in San Diego when we sweated out the broken jaw operation, rode back numb with pleasure and fulfillment and virtually unable to speak.

Soon it began to rain, at first a few drops, then a downpour of almost monsoon proportions. The people thinned out, but still here and there would be families under corrugated tin sheets, waving and smiling.

Meanwhile back at the stadium, when the rains came, they washed out rows of seats, poured through temporary roof and washed parts of that away, disrupted the satellite connections, and flooded the dressing rooms. If the rains had struck one hour sooner, we might have had the first major fight suspended for reasons of weather in the history of the game.

We trooped into Angelo's villa, sat down, and had large brandies to celebrate, but, in truth, we were all too exhausted to do anything but mouth platitudes and start packing our gear for an early escape from Zaire. Angelo and I walked over to Ali's adjoining villa to say goodbye.

Ali was draped over a large chair, reliving the fight, still refighting rounds, and doing his show biz number for the press.

Ali stopped me and broke out into his engaging smile. "We did it, didn't we, Doc? We did it."

We both had a semi-chuckle-laugh over this bit of boasting, and said our goodbyes. Angelo went into a brief conference with him, and we headed out the door to Air Zaire and the ever beating tom-toms.

My luggage arrived in time for me to depart for London one week later, and balancing the good against the bad, I was more than grateful to have been part of this scene. In its uniqueness and its dramatic finish, it had to be the greatest fight scene I had ever been involved in. So far.

PART FOUR

Fight to the Finish

11·The Chilla of a Thrilla in Manila with a Gorilla

OCTOBER 1975

The trip to Manila started out with the usual transportation foulup, when I arrived in San Francisco to find that Delta in Miami had torn off the rest of my trip ticket. Since I had a three-hour layover I was not concerned, and while the Philippine air manager turned his full attention to this matter, I turned to the important matters of the day on the tube: Oakland beating the Dolphins, 31–21, and President Ford, 2, would-be assassins, 0.

The trip was uneventful and the arrival pleasant, and we checked into a dilapidated Hilton without any difficulties.

The coffee shop was beginning to fill up with the advance guard of the Ali retinue, the regulars who came with Ali two or three weeks ahead of time. Through the past two years each man had established his position, but he was likely to pick up a duplicate or clone who was fighting for his job. Angelo Dundee had a new threat in the form of Dick Sadler, the former manager of Foreman. Sadler did such a brainy job of training Foreman that Ali hired him for Manila. Not only was this an unnecessary slap at Angelo, reputed to be the best boxing brain in the world, but it was highly expensive. Sadler, to compound the felony, now insisted he had to return to the

147

U.S.A. for a trial, and took off with a two-way ticket. Cost: two thousand two hundred forty-five dollars. Also, he needed some spending money for the trip, of course. Ali doled it out cheerfully.

Bundini Brown, the soul and semicontrolled hysteric of our camp, has any number of hangers-on, but they vary with each trip and cannot get a good grip on bumping off the mercurial Bundini, who has a hustler's instinct for survival.

Youngblood has seen the light and converted to the Muslim faith. His name, he solemnly tells you, is Wali Muhammad.

"Too bad," I say. "I just made you a great corner jacket with 'Blood' written on the front in red letters."

"It took years for people to learn how to call Ali Ali and not Clay. Why should it take less for them to learn I am Wali and not Blood?" His smooth handsome face broke out in a grin and he deftly accommodated his religious beliefs to the expediency of the moment and tried on his new jacket. His hanger-on was solicitously eyeing the jacket, but he was bush league in this arena.

We used to rely on Luis Sarria to do all the massaging, and he has two advantages: (1) he is sphinx-like and does not talk; and (2) he has the world's greatest hands. If he could talk, his first words would undoubtedly be: "Yassuh." Ali pays him well but keeps him on total alert. Like a Strategic Air Command bomber pilot, Sarria is at twenty-four-hour, everyday call. This trip, in a landmark compromise that rivals the Dred Scott decision in importance, it had been decreed that Sarria will massage the anterior part of the body, and Sadler the posterior aspects, drawing the uppermost borders at the clavicle and the lateral borders at the latissimus Dorsi.

In the field of law we had three attorneys, one in current disrepute, one in limbo, and one in the corner giving the champ water and, I suppose, legal advice. This intrusion into the boxing territory prompted Blood to mutter angrily at him, "Get your mother-grabbing hands off my water bottle. You don't see me in *your* court handling *your* briefs."

I also had a clone in the form of a doctor from Chicago who was Herbert's family doctor, and he was invited to Zaire as a guest. The good doctor brought his bag and became a fixture in each camp, unobtrusively giving aid and comfort. Herbert took his time to explain to me that he was only a guest, and not meant to interfere in my end as a boxer's doctor. But he convinced Ali that he had hypoglycemia in Africa, and prepared a huge pie with honey for him to eat before the fight. Fortunately, that was short-circuited. However, that "put some gas in the gas tank" approach has hung on ever since and I find, to my dismay, that the dressing room contains a huge box of creamy pastries for Ali to consume before stepping out into the pressure cooler of the Manila Colosseum and Joe Frazier. I handled this deftly by eating them mostly myself, and feeding the rest to our human disposal unit, the rotund Hassan, an informant and general counterintelligence man for Herbert.

The good doctor from Chicago finished off the Manila caper with a flourish. He sent Herbert a substantial bill for his services as an invited guest.

Behind the first-string working crew came the business managers, of whom the most unlikely and most tenaciously successful had to be a large Irish tumulter named Gene Kilroy. Kilroy is an original and had no clone. Gene was the only white man in camp except for Angelo and me. He survived up in the Pennsylvania mountains with Ali and his group, and the champ is genuinely fond of Gene because he recognizes a soulmate in the game of divide and conquer. He loves to see Gene agitate the camp one against the other. Next to him Iago looks like Tricia Nixon. He is an endlessly complicated man, one minute a brooding worrier of Welshian proportions. One of his main pastimes is photographing nudes, from girl bellhops in Cleveland to cocktail waitresses in Vegas. He has them filed alphabetically in a shoebox, and although I must admit it is better than looking at old fight films, still one can see only so much before a panoramic view of multiple T & A turns your brain to mush. Gene gets uptight fast, and even a slight kidding question as to his machismo, which certainly isn't a real question at all, can sometimes throw him into an Irish fury.

In Vegas for the Lyle fight, I invited Shirley MacLaine to the workout and she graciously came, then went to lunch with Gentleman Harold Conrad and me. Gene soon joined us and began a long recitation of his sexual conquests of the last few days, mentioning enough names to fill a Ziegfeld cast. The penetratingly shrewd Shirley punctuated the list with a quiet remark. "Why don't you try a boy in that lineup. You may like it."

Gene laughed that one off, and to this fight he brought a lovely girl named Betsy, and stayed relatively quiet.

The other business manager was "talent scout" Lloyd Wells, who in another life was a top NFL scout for Hank Stram and the Kansas City Chiefs. Lloyd, in his own words, was now a talent scout for Ali, on the lookout for "wide receivers." A huge man with a shark-like restlessness, on the prowl in the lobby from dawn to dawn, possessed with some pelvic demon that forced him to "nail down the action." He is partly deaf, which may play a great part in his success as a seducer, and given to graphic descriptions of girls. As one of his victims came by, he said, "She gives General Motors head." I was left to wonder whether that was a qualitative or quantitative description.

C. B. Atkins and Richard Durham were a pair that are hard to describe. C. B.'s previous claim to fame was that he had courted and married a variety of singers, including the Divine One, Sarah Vaughan. He was always on the scene making large deals with the locals for copper and diamonds, and forming international cartels. He has driven many an emerging nation back into economic oblivion.

Durham had been writing his Ali book for the past four years. It was said to be almost completed now, but Herbert noticed a few strange things in the four-hundred-plus pages. For instance, Herbert is barely mentioned, but Don King is mentioned a lot. A big part of Ali's boxing life is Angelo Dundee, but he had only two paragraphs in the book. C. B. Atkins was mentioned a lot. Rewriting took up most of Durham's time in Manila.

The city of Chicago loaned us Pat Patterson, a tough, big cop who was now Ali's protection against the snatch-and-stab boys. His clone was his lieutenant, Lucius, whom I recommended to Herbert as *his* bodyguard, since Herbert is almost as valuable to abductors as Ali himself. They were tough and surly as only big city black cops can be.

The rest of the hard-core camp consisted of Coretta, the cook, a sweet, gentle relative of Ali's and a General Motors cook, and Lana Shabazz, a tough cookie of the "what-have-you-done-for-me-lately-Honkie" school.

In camp for the first time was a butler (and his wife) picked up in Malaysia, a minister (Baptist) who had the church Ali used to go to in another life, a fat man whose claim to the camp is that he fell off Ali's bike as a kid and has limped since, thereby obligating Ali in some fashion for the remainder of his life. The rest of the faithful brothers would arrive daily until we filled the roster of the camp to over fifty hard-charging followers.

The workers of the camp also included the photographers, Howard Bingham, Tony, and Potter, Herbert's secretaries, and the dark, brooding Lowell Riley who, along with Bingham, had been with the Ali Circus since the beginning.

In Africa, Don King sent over four beauty finalists in a Black America Pageant to juice up the promotion. I don't know what it did for the promotion but it certainly did juice up Ali, who spotted a tall beauty named Veronica and moved her into the camp.

What started as a mild altercation with wife Belinda developed into some moderate physical force being used, and finally resulted in an expensive trip for Belinda to Paris to put things right.

Somehow Veronica hung in there and Ali, a very persuasive man and a charmer with the ladies, managed to have Belinda accept this new aid and comfort as a babysitter and/or relative. In time they came to dress alike and even to hold hands going to the fights in Cleveland, Vegas, and Malaysia.

Buoyed up by this apparent victory, Ali overstepped his bounds in Manila and introduced Veronica to the president as his wife. Thereafter, the Philippine newspapers referred to her as his number one wife and, upon Belinda's arrival, called her his *other* wife.

The problem, then, as any fan of the thirties comedies can see, was one of *billing*. Belinda had come to accept being a number two wife, but not replacement at the top billing, name-above-the-title spot. She flew in in a rage, and left in a huff. Total flying time, twenty-six hours in. Total rage time, fifteen minutes.

Ali was immovable. He reviewed his financial contributions to her welfare, and she pointed out a few facts not on a ledger sheet. She roared out and he opened the door to let her pass, since she is a black belt and given to shattering doors as a means of gaining egress from a room.

I spoke to her briefly, urging her not to go, but since she was quite correct in her position of number one wife, and mother of his four children, all arguments were rather weak, and ultimately she left for the airport where customs men fainted at the prospect of reopening twenty-four bags they had just inspected minutes before.

Shortly thereafter Ali had a serious altercation with his

mother, and that seemed a bad omen for the fight since he felt that the two women who meant most to him had let him down in a real moment of need.

To most mortals, having your number one wife walk out on you, and having a fiery argument with your beloved mother, would be very bothersome. Add the thought of facing a Smoking Joe Frazier, full of pent-up animosity and frustration, and Ali should have been shaken up, but such is not the makeup of this iron-willed champion. Typically, he turned the news around to himself, and left the situation and his opponent in some dark, hidden corner, to be trotted out in the light when Ali saw fit.

The dinosaurs of boxing were now working feverishly in the backrooms and bars to "protect their fighter." What exactly does that mean? Haggling over ring size, ropes, corners, tape measures, rules, scoring, and, above all, securing the "right" referee. The promotion brought over two Americans (one black, one white) and an Englishman. All are acceptable to us for one reason or another. Futch, Frazier's manager, won't have Zack Clayton, the black, for reasons best known to himself. He is not too crazy about Jay Edson (he lives in Florida with the Dundees), and the Englishman is a friend of Jarvis who is a friend of Ali. Moves are made, countermoves devised. Who will be the ref?

They finally decide a small Filipino ref will be the one. And so it goes. The fight approaches and the real and *only* test will begin.

They were up at six in the morning. The sun was out, with the local TV showing all of Ali's fights in full for the past two years. Our camp was up, and the coffee shop full of the prefight hysteria, centered mainly around who had what ticket, and how were all the Faithful going to get to the fight.

At eight, President Marcos announced that the fight would be shown, live, free, on home TV as a gift from the president on channels 7 and 9 which, by some odd coincidence, happened to be owned by the president's wife. Outside traffic came to a standstill as everyone ran for a TV set.

Inside the Colosseum, Angelo had a fighter getting killed by Larry Holmes. We got the word that they were out of stuff to stop bleeding, and I rushed up in time to see Bobick leave the world of the conscious.

The ringside had that same electric tension that all Ali-Frazier fights have. Perhaps it was not as intense as the first fight, which was truly about as high voltage as electricity gets, and perhaps the array of names was not as lustrous (we did have Norman Mailer, Flip Wilson, Hugh O'Brian, and most of the pimps and high-rollers of Detroit, Chicago, and Cleveland), but the sellout crowd did not know that and, with the appearance of Ali in a shining white robe, they went wild.

Frazier was in a denim robe and trunks, grim, tight-lipped, dedicated, smoldering, and above all ready. He could barely choke out a "Hi, Doc" when I went over to watch them glove up and I must say I uttered a prayer that he not be hurt in this, which might be his final fight. Joe is a decent man, much loved in boxing, and a man easy to admire. He had his share of followers and they were loud in their cheers of Frazier! Frazier! Ali feigned amazement and gawked at the crowd.

Ali was still clowning as they introduced in the center of the ring a small man bearing a huge multilayered statue. This was to be presented to the winner of the bout. Ali tiptoed out and stole it back to his corner. The crowd roared with laughter and Frazier looked as if he had taken a hard right to the heart.

The fight itself was a thing of fistic beauty, divided into three stages:

Stage 1. Ali trying for a quick KO. Fast-footed and punching with authority, Ali got Joe into real trouble in the second round and kept coming at him like Grant after Lee in the wilderness.

Stage 2. From round five on, Ali tired and tried his Africa trick of letting Joe bombard him with his heaviest artillery. This almost backfired when Ali got caught with some devastating hooks that glazed over his eyes, but Ali, for all his slick good looks, is as tough a man as any gargoyle punching bag, and he has a great ability to take a punch.

Stage 3. Joe had worn himself out punching to Ali's rock-like body. Ali was exhausted too, but he has that extra kick in his tank that champions need. Ali sensed Joe's weakness. Now he began a war of movement which Joe's benumbed legs couldn't follow. Joe stumbled forth, absorbing lightning jabs. He began to look like a tank lumbering under a rocket attack from fighter planes. His facial tissues couldn't withstand the assault and began to swell, clouding his vision. The taste of blood was in his mouth and at one point, after a devastating right cross, his mouthpiece sailed into the third row and a long slobber of bloody saliva drooled from his mouth. The comparison to a bull before the kill flashed through my mind, and we began screaming to the ref to stop the fight. The fourteenth round was more of the same, and now even the crowd, not known for its compassion in a fight arena, began to chant for a stopping of the fight.

I looked over to Eddie Futch, saw his worried face, and knew that Joe wouldn't come out for the fifteenth. Eddie, one of the rare humane managers, felt that Joe was ahead but couldn't continue, and he stopped the fight. That was highly commendable and unspeakably brave, for if there is anything odious to fight people it is to stop a fight prematurely, especially if one is ahead at the time, and if it's for the big one. Joe wanted to go on, since he has a fighter's heart and doesn't know the meaning of the word "quit."

In our corner we were delirious. Ali fell to the floor to avoid the crunch. Filipino cops sealed off the ring, pushing back, at one point, the closed-circuit cameraman, which left Don Dunphy standing in the center of the ring doing radio bits on television.

No one else was allowed in Ali's room at the Hilton after the fight, but I walked in to examine the champ. He is in bed exhausted, small purple marks under both eyes and angry, red hematomas on both hips, where Joe landed those sledge-hammer hooks to the side. He looks at me with that half smile and says, "You think Joe got my heart in Manila, or did I get Joe's heart?"

"You got his heart and his ass too in Manila, Champ."

Ali waves a good-humored, give-me-five hand slap, and sighs, "I hope that's the last I ever have to see of Joe Frazier."

Uttering a silent amen, I tiptoe out of the room and back into the world of mere mortals.

12·Diary of a Downhill Ride— The Last Norton Fight

SEPTEMBER 1976

Veterans of Napoleon's armies spent the rest of their lives speaking with reverence the names of their past glorious fields of combat: Marengo, Austerlitz, Jaffa, Shubra Khit, Vilna, and Borodino.

Like Napoleon's veterans, the veterans of the Ali Circus speak fondly of Kuala Lumpur, Manila, Show-Low, Munich, Tokyo, Kinshasa, Deer Lake, Dakarta, Frankfurt, London, and Zurich. Now the Battle of Yankee Stadium will be talked about with the same sorrow with which the French speak of Waterloo, and the rebels of Gettysburg.

This was the night that Ali stopped being Ali. It was the night all fighters dread, the night when the body can no longer do what the mind dictates. When thoughts cannot be translated into instant action, when reflexes fail, and the body begins to *feel* the punishment and the exhaustion. When old talents fail, and when all that is left is guile, experience, cunning, and the *will to win*.

It is a well-known boxing adage that the boxer is the last to know when to retire, but Ali could never be classified as just another boxer. Ali has always maintained that *he* would know and would quit without persuasion.

157

What follows is a diary of events leading up to the sad night of September 28, 1976, starting with my arrival in New York City six days before to attend the Ali-Norton title fight. In order to describe the atmosphere of a fight week in New York City I must relate all events sequentially, so that the reader may understand the crazy treadmill one is caught on while trying to satisfy everyone's needs. If the following seems to be an exercise in name dropping, the reader should realize that there is no way to describe a fight scene without the obligatory names. If it bothers you, cross out the names and substitute members of your family instead. Can I help it if Ali draws the biggies?

SEPTEMBER 22—WEDNESDAY

After a hectic run through a hospital and two office visits, I caught a late flight to New York with my wife Luisita, hoping to make it in time for a quick supper and the long-awaited show *Chorus Line*. My wife worked as a flamenco dancer for many years and now has a flamenco academy with the great Spanish dancer, Jose Molina. His manager, Arthur Sharfman, in appreciation for past favors, had reserved two seats for us. Luisita was more excited about this than about the upcoming fight. Dancers have one-track minds.

A few hours later we walked out into the street in a numbed condition, exhilarated by the magic of the play which had a special significance for Luisita, since she lived through those experiences and now had a torn cartilage which was preventing her from dancing at the moment. We walked to the Warwick Hotel, lost in the pleasant cool air and the smells of Manhattan, reliving the last few hours of pure theatrical joy. As we walked up to the hotel entrance, arm in arm, a drab shambles of a man in his mid-sixties came stag-

158

gering up. He held forth a tattered chrysanthemum with a broken stem, and offered it to Luisita, who took it gracefully.

With foul breath he spoke. *"Times Square should be times crooked."*

We watched as he doddered down Fifty-fourth Street, and looked at each other. "Welcome to New York," I said, and we both laughed.

SEPTEMBER 23—THURSDAY

The alarm rings at seven and I hop into some warm clothes, don my Ali jacket (with a bee and a butterfly on the back) and stumble out of the lobby into a waiting cab.

The cab has its trunk open and full of luggage. The cabbie looks at my sophomoric attire malevolently, and grunts a "Where to?" like an insult.

"East Sixty-second Street," I say, knowing instinctively that this will cause the kind of trouble that I don't need at seven-thirty in the morning.

"What! East Sixty-second! My luck! Been waiting all morning for my turn and I get a ride just across the park!"

What followed was more descriptive than truly obscene but I dropped into the plastic cell that the back seats of New York cabs have become, and tried to turn my mind off.

We arrived in front of Bob Arum's apartment and I got out with the fare in hand. The cab driver, still muttering darkly, ran to the trunk and started to unload luggage. I watched in amusement as it dawned on me that I was about to enjoy the rarest of moments accorded to lucky individuals once in a lifetime: to have the last laugh on a New York cabbie.

"Hold on, pal, that luggage is not mine."

A blank expression, then the faint glimmer of realization, and the cabbie points to the luggage. "These ain't yours? Say, ain't you the guy that called for a cab at the Warwick at seven-thirty?"

"No, and if you had been thinking instead of cussing you might be halfway out to Kennedy now instead of on the East Side."

I laughed as I got into Arum's car with a lady correspondent from *Sports Illustrated* named Paula, and as we pulled off I saw the worried cabbie talking on the phone and gesticulating wildly. For once I had gotten my own back on a New York City cabbie.

The air was cold and the countryside beautiful as we drove north into the Catskills. The leaves were turning the entire area into the natural masterpiece Nature intended. The conversation with Arum was spirited, as it always is with this dynamic attorney-promoter with whom I feel a strange kinship. We had both started as young professional men, he a lawyer and I a doctor, both white men with the Ali Circus. Now here we were years later, much farther up the professional and social ladder, and, above all, survivors of the Ali Wars. The young reporter sat quietly immersed in her own thoughts, half listening to our old war stories and seemingly lost in the beauty of the countryside, laughing at inappropriate places, and nodding absently.

Bob Arum had suggested that I be present, at the commission physical which is a pure formality and ritual, but I had agreed in order to see Ali, Angelo, and the gang, and to let them know I had arrived. In the Ali Circus you arrive when you can, no one misses you if you are late.

On the way to Grossinger's we passed Norton out for a walk and stopped to greet him.

I admire Ken Norton as a person, boxer, and sportsman.

He is a likable, handsome man unimpressed by his show biz and athletic successes, and I have always maintained a camaraderie with him in spite of the fact that I work hard for his defeat. This day he breaks out with his flashing smile. "Hi, Doc, take care of *The Man*."

"Luck, Ken," I say as he strolls off without further chitchat, intent on concentrating on the task ahead. Ali is his nemesis, but he is also Ali's nemesis.

Grossinger's is Norton's hotel. In a typical move, Ali has chosen it for the physical. Nothing Ali does is ever predictable. Ali wants a platform, and Norton's camp seems to be the place to invade. Shades of the Liston fight? Reliving the first Frazier fight? Will those old ploys work? Will Norton fall for this old stuff? Can he still be susceptible to the ancient ploys? Norton says no. We shall see.

John X. Condon, the Irish Prussian from Madison Square Garden, is laying out the course the physical exam will take. He is on a small platform, indicating to the photographers where to stand, and pointing to rows of chairs where the newsmen will sit.

"When the fighters get through with Dr. Nardiello you photographers will have a full fifteen minutes for your pictures. After that you news guys got 'em for another half hour. Let's get this straight: the photographers have to leave after their fifteen minutes. No hanging around!"

I smile serenely at John X., knowing his cogent precise plan is meaningless since Ali and the Faithful Fifty will make a shambles of the proceedings. Let's get this straight: John X. Condon is the best in the world at what he does, managing the press, but he is as helpless as anyone else in the world when managing Ali's Circus on the warpath.

Dr. Nardiello is a kind, quiet, small man, courteous and likable, and he smiles at me knowing also that Ali will not do things simply but will put on a production.

Norton comes in first and is examined in private. What is shown to the press will be sham for publicity. He is quiet and pensive, but then we all rush to the windows when we hear a roar. Ali and the Faithful Fifty have arrived.

Ali, dressed in black, as is his custom, enters first carrying a sign: NORTON MUST FALL. A small Italian man with a huge cowboy hat carries another: KNOCK HIM O.U.T. This is Angelo Dundee, the only man to be with Ali at the beginning, and the only real boxing man in the group apart from old, serious, quiet Luis Sarria who shuffles in on bad gunboat flat feet, smiling but carrying no sign. They are followed by Bundini, the camp cheerleader and spiritual witch doctor, Youngblood (now *Wali*), Patterson the bodyguard, Kilroy and Lloyd Wells, and other members all carrying placards and wearing cowboy hats. The rear is brought up by Dick Sadler with a mysterious black box. Arum drily observes that only in boxing could the ex-manager of the deposed champion be taken in by the man who took his title away without summoning up a full-scale congressional investigation.

Norton is not amused. Ali is just getting warmed up, and the voice is getting into good form when John X. attempts to restore order.

"Ali! Only you and *one* man will be allowed when you take your physical. Then, when you are through, you pose with Norton for the boys for ten minutes, then questions . . ."

John X. doesn't finish because the Faithful have seeped onto every nook and cranny of the creaking platform. Ali is shouting and being restrained by Angelo, which in itself is some sight since Ali is six foot three and Angelo is five foot seven after being stretched on a rack. Bundini, second only to Ali in vocal vituperation and inventiveness, is booming insults into his opposite number in Norton's group.

162

John X. tries to hold Bundini. "Now stop this, Bundini, or I'll have to throw you out!"

Ali stops his apparently uncontrollable tirade and whispers into John X.'s ear. "Don't pay him no attention. Don't make him *big*. He ain't nothing. Don't make him *big*."

Ah, show biz! It's always a question of billing. Ali is the star of this show and don't you forget it.

Now Norton is getting hot at Bundini who is pawing his shoulder, "Don't touch me, punk, don't ever touch me!"

Again Ali leans in to Norton. "Don't make him *big,* man!"

Now Bundini has used up his considerable stock of insults and Norton has reached a block, and they stare at each other, minds busting for a single, final riposte. A KO verbal punch. An end-all punctuation, and Bundini of the street tongue wins the race. "And . . . and . . . I can *out-act* you too!"

Felled by that arrow to the center of his ego, Norton falls back and out of sight, leaving the doctor to examine Ali. Ali is still yelling as the doctor places the stethoscope to his chest. The doctor's eyes revolve in his head as if he tuned in to Niagara Falls falling on a giant kettle drum. A stethoscope on Ali's chest when he is at full pitch is an eardrum blower. His pressure must be 200/100 but the seasoned doctor calmly calls out, "120/80, Ali in excellent condition."

John X. has a worried look on his face. *The Plan* is not working. Flashbulbs explode in his face, reporters with tape recorders stick mikes in Ali's face, cords are draped over John X.'s Irish nose. Is this any way to run a quiet prefight physical?

Finally, mercifully, it is over. Norton leaves. Ali and the over-the-hill mob leaves, but not before Ali sends Sadler over to Norton with his box. In the box is a black cat for Norton, who hates cats, especially black ones.

On the ride back I get to talk to my old and dear English friend, writer and TV commentator Reggie Gutteridge, who has two great surprises for me. One is a smashing RAF beret owned by the King's personal pilot. Reggie, knowing I collect military headgear, always brings me a nifty gift. The other surprise is his even more smashingly beautiful 21-year-old daughter, who is studying literature and thinking of a career in journalism.

The girl is impressed by the Ali Circus. Lloyd Wells, the former Kansas City Chiefs scout, and now an Ali scout, has already hit on her, to Reggie's considerable consternation. This day Reggie is moving her to New York City and I am able to reciprocate for his many kindnesses and give him my two tickets to *Chorus Line*. How can we allow this charming girl to leave our shores thinking all of the U.S.A. is like the Catskills?

Arum makes a date for lunch to talk about this book, and I get to the Warwick in time to dress for supper and take Luisita to a great Spanish restaurant—Torremolinos.

The world of the flamencos is small. As we walk in we hear a tremendous flamenco guitarist who is singing in fine voice a flamenco rumba. "Domingo Alvarado! It's got to be!" And, sure enough, Luisita and Domingo are in an excited conversation in Spanish, and I am deep into my zarzuela. That night I had no difficulty falling asleep. I was listening to the Presidential Debates.

SEPTEMBER 24—FRIDAY

This day I met my literary agent Jed Mattes who came to lunch with Bob Arum in order to discuss business pertaining to my book. Jed appeared to be a neat, young, intelligent man, who listened well and contributed his knowhow when asked. We set some plans to meet the man from Simon and Schuster and broke up so that I could drive to the Concord and spend the night with the Ali Circus before breaking camp.

After a light lunch I rented a car and, with a road map and my wife's infallible sense of direction, we struck out for the Concord. The ride was nice and soon we pulled up to the door of the golf clubhouse, as a huge sparring partner came out laden with equipment.

Rodney Bobick was wearing his Minnesota Vikings shirt, and had large lumps on his face. "Hi, Doc, Angie is in there. We are just going in to the city."

"What? I just got here to spend the night."

Angelo came out to the car with a half smile on his face, and muttered a good-natured hello. "I tried to call you not to come but it was already too late. You had left. Oh, well, now you can take us back after supper."

The Ali camp was slowly coming to the table. Ali was at the head of a large one. He smiled when he saw me and shook my hand, and his smile lit up the room. "We ready now. You come to another big fight, huh Doc? You really don't miss a fight, do you Doc?"

I was beginning to feel like a fan instead of Ali's doctor for the past fifteen years. I really never got past the idea that Ali thinks I am there as a spectator rather than as a worker. This is especially confusing, since I work in his corner during the fight.

Over at another table sat Martha Louis, Joe's wife, holding Ali's youngest daughter, six-week-old Hana, waiting for Veronica to come down and join them. We sat with her a moment and Ali came over and gently took the baby from Martha's hands. As he sat gently cuddling her and kissing her upturned face, Luisita broke out her new Canon camera and began to snap a series of what should have been memorable pictures, except that in her inexperience with the new camera she forgot to wind it properly.

As soon as we got through eating with Alex Ben Block and

his wife, Jodie, newly hired as the sports editor for a Detroit newspaper, we got Angelo and Sarria in the car and started out for the road. But we were intercepted by Ali, who asked us to take Jeremiah and Lloyd back to Manhattan. There being bad blood between Jeremiah and Lloyd, we eventually got to take only one back—Lloyd.

A trip with Lloyd Wells is an experience in the infinite varieties of the English language, since Lloyd always has colorful descriptions and unusual insights into situations that seem routine. I offer two examples:

In referring to obtaining tickets for some of the lesser members of the entourage he referred to *parachute seats,* which he finally deciphered for me as twenty-five-dollar seats in the upper decks of Yankee Stadium. His explanation was: "Then if they want to come into the ring they will have to use parachutes."

The other observation came after we had passed the fifth tollgate on the way into New York. "I can see why no Mexican ever makes it into the city."

The promotion had furnished fifty rooms at the Statler Hilton, but Ali and a few of the Faithful Fifty checked into the Essex Marriott, the net result being that the fifty rooms at the Statler remained mainly empty while the Essex Marriott bulged with the extra load. A note for the accountants: the Statler rooms were free, while the Essex rooms were on Ali's private bill. No one seemed to mind.

SEPTEMBER 25—SATURDAY

Ali is finding the Essex too popular as his army congregates in the lobby and maneuvers for tickets and free accommodations. The foxes are also in layers in the halls, and Ali has been abstemious for twenty-two days, which means that his resolve cannot hold out much longer. Ali decides to go to the mattress, in the gangland sense, and he picks Harold Conrad's apartment to hide in. Harold Conrad is a sharp old-time New York fight guy. He has promoted, written sports, done publicity, and in general done everything in fighting except fight. He is married to a dancer-actress who follows all the fights with him, and she is an addition to any camp with her sharp looks and sharp wit. Ali will not be bored with Mara and Conrad doing the entertaining. Most important is the fact that few of the entourage know the whereabouts of the Conrad apartment, and his phone is unlisted. Ali goes into hiding and the shuffle for the tickets and freebies goes on.

This morning Angelo and I have a rare moment alone and he lays a bomb on me. Ali in a thoughtless moment picked his corner: Angelo, Bundini, Sarria, and Rahaman (Ali's brother). John X. wants verification so that he can bar everyone else from the corner. It would seem that Angelo himself could speak up and rectify this error, but at this point in the Ali career Angelo is powerless to do anything about it, so he bleakly informs me to consult Herbert about this obvious error.

I hurry to Herbert's apartment, which is located on the corner by the Essex House, and Angelo wants to come with me, but at the last moment thinks better of it and leaves me to talk to Herbert alone. That is the way I prefer it, since Herbert is a very fair, no-nonsense kind of man, and I never need help in talking for myself. Herbert comes down to the lobby and we sit and talk while an envoy from Egypt waits in another corner of the lobby.

Herbert is visibly upset by the article Mark Kram did on him in the current *Sports Illustrated* and we talk quietly for ten minutes about this until Herbert comes to the point, saying, "Haven't I always surrounded Ali by the best boxing people? Angelo is the best cornerman in boxing, you are the best boxing doctor, Bundini and Blood are the best and most trustworthy men I know."

"Why then are you replacing Blood and me, or is that just a mistake?" He seems startled and says it is obviously a mistake and he will straighten it out in a moment, which he does as soon as he goes over to the Essex House and sees Ali. Blood hears about it after it is all straightened out, and he is insulted and hurt, but it is all over in a minute when he finds out it has been straightened out by the straight-shooting Herbert. As in all of my dealings with Herbert, he has performed admirably, getting to the heart of the matter in a moment. Another tempest in a teapot out of the way.

The ticket situation is now getting ludicrous as I have about four thousand dollars' worth of tickets out, and supposedly bought by people who are not appearing to repay me. Seat position is very important, and I find Norman Lear two tickets in the eleventh row through Arum, which I have to get to him in his suite at the Essex.

Norman Lear is a witty, down-to-earth, humane guy who has not let Hollywood success go to his balding, graying head. He laughs freely and is very obliging to writers, photographers, and the public in general. He seems happy as a kid to get his tickets, but he too has no money to repay me and seems embarrassed until his excellent secretary Jadie Joe comes in with her personal check. He has as his guest the editor of the *Washington Post,* who does not look at all like Jason Robards.

I have been trying to get a free ringsider for my gynecologist friend, Dr. Gus Moreno, who furnishes us with hospital accommodations at Flower Fifth, when we need it with fighters in New York. To date I do not have time even to see this old friend, and as it turns out never do get to see him, much less give him his free ticket.

Night comes too rapidly and I have a date to take Petula Clark to a restaurant of her choice. I am also entertaining (the late) Tom Gries, the director of the film on Ali (*The*

Greatest), and his wife Sally. In the lobby we run across his teenage son John 'who is in New York to study with Stella Adler and do the starvation bit, so we take him with us to eat. The meal is joyous and the conversation good, then we decide to walk down Broadway, and Petula is radiant in her happiness since, as she observes, this is a rare treat to walk down a crowded street with the stores open and the happy blacks yelling at her and laughing and enjoying a Saturday stroll along Broadway to Times Square. The blacks notice us more than the whites, and Petula gets the most attention— after her Tom Gries, who looks like a cross between Kojak and Yul Brynner, and even a few of the fight fans recognize me from the Ali publicity. At one corner Tom meets an ebullient, loud actor fresh from the Montefuscos TV series, and the corner turns into a sideshow. I can't help wondering if the people around me realize the array of talent gathered on that corner. We could have really put on a show with Petula singing, Luisita dancing and the actor entertaining as Tom Gries directs. While we stand and laugh I feel eager hands searching for my pocket and wallet. *Times Square is indeed times crooked.*

We drop off Petula and head for Eddie Condon's to hear a good Dixie Land band, led by the ancient, wheezing, emphysematous trombone of Vic Dickenson, and still a thing of beauty. Fight three days away now.

SEPTEMBER 26—SUNDAY

The blissful silence of Sunday in New York greets us as we hit the streets to join everyone at the Stage Delicatessen for a late breakfast. Ali is safely ensconced in his haven with only a brief trip scheduled to Gleason's Gym to work out and, aside from the fresh arrivals, the day looks trouble-free.

Noon, and the usual hectic scramble for places in limos going to the workout ensues. As usual, the workers get shut out of these accommodations, but today we have a special ride in *Black Beauty,* Bundini's '76 Eldorado. Angelo, Blood, Sarria, and I head for the ratty gym on the West Side, close to where the old Garden used to be, in a very rough area. Gleason's is a perfectly preserved relic of the twenties-thirties days of fighting, small and smelly. By comparison, the Fifth Street Gym of Miami is the Taj Mahal. Ali swarms in with his clot of followers. The caretaker has instructions not to let *anyone* in for the workout from the rigid John X., who has decreed against even family members. Ali will toil only for the eyes of the press. Nice try, John X. The joint is swarming with relatives and assorted hangers-on, and John X. is pushed to the wall by the mass of humanity.

In a corner, working quietly with only the old Freddie Brown to watch him is perhaps the greatest active champion fighting today: that small, compact bundle of destructive energy, Roberto Duran, preparing for a Miami title fight. He seems bemused by the entire panoply of the Ali Circus. He methodically destroys the heavy bag, and even the seasoned Freddie Brown winces as the little man rearranges the sand of the heavy bag with his siege gun hammering blows. Duran is a thing of destructive beauty. Once Ali was the very best in the world, and the best of all time. Now in the other elevated ring Ali is heavily sliding around in a pathetic imitation of the young Cassius Clay, floating like a butterfly. Watching him closely this lazy Sunday morning, my mind goes back to a quote by a famous Mexican caricaturist of the Impressionist Era at the turn of the century. When asked by Picasso who was the greatest caricaturist of the ages, the Mexican answered simply, "Time."

And so this 34-year-old caricature of *The Greatest* was going through his motions, most of the changes undetected by the loving eyes of his trainers and cornermen and followers and idolators. These changes come so slowly, and the pattern of win, win, win, win erases all doubts that he is still *The Greatest* and the best. The Muslim yes men were still punctuating Ali's remarks with their staccato exhortations of *"Yeah, brother, yeah!"* and *"Preach, brother!"* and *"Right on, brother!"* and laughing at the right places and trying to catch his eye for a flick of a moment, or pat him as he walks by or in some way touch him. He is a lavishly loved man.

The crowd is now pushed into a tight semicircle around the work area, with the reporters sweating hard for some fresh slant on tomorrow's story, trying to rearrange Ali's diatribes to sound fresh even though they have been writing about this man for fifteen years and there *are* no fresh quotes, no fresh ideas. The newsmen work frantically interviewing the cornermen. Angelo is always helpful and can usually be counted on for a good quote or two. Bundini is a fountainhead of inventive street talk, and in desperation they turn to me for some wise doctorly evaluations of the ravages of time on a 34-year-old athlete's body. Now Ali senses that his act is getting stale, and he pauses for a minute studying the crowd with his devilish, bemused expression that I know means that it is *funny time* in his mind. The reporters spot this and wait, pencils poised for the first line like the NBC Symphony waiting for the downbeat of Toscanini's baton.

"Dick Young!" Ali bellows in a mock angry tone, then with his winning sly smile he easily starts his monologue. "I like you, man, you tough on me. Write that trash, Dick Young, you just make me fight harder to make you look bad. Dick Young. *Doc* Young, in Chicago, writes bad about me, *and he is a brother!* Dick Young, keep writing that stuff, man, I love it—you keeping me fighting hard. Poor ole Norton gonna get it cause Dick Young been writing I am through."

On and on it goes for a full fifteen minutes while the

writers, including a beaming Dick Young, scramble to scribble every word as if they were hearing this for the very *first* time. Occasionally Dave Anderson of the *Times* or Vic Seigel of the *Post* would look at me and half smile, half wince, but go back to scribbling. It beats working.

In the upper gallery is most of Angelo Dundee's immediate family. His lovely wife Helen and their incongruously tall six-foot-three-inch son Jimmy, come to experience a last hurrah. Angelo's competent secretary Betty, who has patiently handled all the Ali details for the past fifteen years but has never been to a fight, has finally come to an Ali match. Friends from Miami accompany them, and they are having bizarre experiences in New York. Dave Rogers' wife Bookie was minding her own business in the hotel when she heard screams in the hallway. Being a nurse, she opened the door and was rewarded by witnessing the fatal stabbing of a man. So she spent the night in the police station answering questions, and must now return to the Big Apple to appear at the inquest. Nothing is ever simple in the Ali camp.

The workout is coming to a close and my wife Luisita is busily working her Canon camera with the technical aid of Tom Gries, who is being hustled by every camp follower to be put into the movie.

Gries and his unit production manager, Tom Shaw, are eating up the fight atmosphere. They are two coast guys that are real macho fight-movie people, and an hour in a smelly gym is tonic to their souls. If they can capture this circus on film they should have an original fight movie.

Ali disappears up the stairs to his dressing cubicle, which also serves as the main (and only) office of this relic gym. The small room is packed with the followers, and I squeeze out to mingle with old friends in the press. Angelo is working hard in a corner giving some German news guys some fresh slants and John X. is busily planning the next set of rules that will be broken. Sadly, he will never learn that this is not the New York Athletic Club Awards Dinner, but the Ali Circus in full bloom.

The weather has turned cold and drizzly. I have visions of Bob Arum in his luxury apartment quietly praying at the altar by his bed. The altar is a huge cash register.

That afternoon is spent watching the Dolphins thrashing about trying to beat an even more inept New York Jets team. Everywhere I look there are washed-up old champions trying to recapture their past glories. Is there no surcease to this queasy premonition I have of impending fistic disaster?

That night there is a huge NBC party to be televised, but I have guests from Miami and want to spend the time with them and Tom and Sally Gries, so I pass up the party and go with my friends to Luchow's. Afterward the night is still young, and Dr. Howard Gordon states that there is time to work in a movie. So the four of us trundle uptown to see a French farce, *Cousin, Cousine,* which, by any of our standards, is not much of a flick.

Next day Helen Dundee outlines the tone of the previous evening at the NBC party when she says she was never served her supper, and the music by a rock group was too loud. I ask her who the rock group was, and she says, "I don't know. It was four names . . ."

"Crosby Stills," I start, but she waves a quick no.

"Four names. Four names. I know. *Blood Sweat and Tears.*" I love Helen Dundee.

SEPTEMBER 27—MONDAY

John Marshall, as usual, has won over John X.'s orderly and resistant spirit by sheer grit and persistence. Columbia Pictures will have their press conference at noon today to announce the movie, and show the two young kids they have discovered to play the young Ali.

The sun never sets on John Marshall. The determined, outrageously cheeky, confident Englishman, who has been working on producing this picture for the past three years, is in rare form. I call him John the Despicable and he seems to enjoy this as part of his tough reputation. He is charming and has a great sense of humor, but he is ruthless in business and can be a terrible bully. He is as persistent and tenacious as the English bulldog and as deadly in financial negotiations as bubonic plague. Today he is in his glory. With a captive New York and world press audience, Ali at his side, and two Columbia bigwigs to observe his production, John Marshall is in his heaven.

The Empire Room at the Essex is packed with newsmen and observers. I sit in the front row with Harold and Mara Conrad to view the spectacle. The conference starts tamely enough, but soon Ali is asked to speak. He starts out slowly enough, but begins to build as his audience responds to his funny stuff. Now he forgets the picture and starts to talk about the upcoming fight, then to *other* projected movies, and projects involving his religion, and somehow the conference gets completely out of hand. Leo Jaffe, chairman of Columbia Pictures, seems amused, being exposed to Ali for the first time, but his partner Allan Hirschfield, president of Columbia Pictures, is more confused than amused. There is a lot of surreptitious looking at diamond-studded wristwatches as the time flies by.

Ali is droning down to a catalogue of his past infirmities which had not permitted him to do well against Norton in past fights. Ali seems to get renewed vigor from this line of thought, and he is once again in high gear which is like catching Senator Claghorn on the rise in a congressional filibuster. Finally he spots me in the first row. "There is my doctor. Dr. Pacheco, come up here. Here is the man that helped me get through all those tough fights when I was having trouble with my hands. Come up here and sit down by me, Doc."

I obediently trudge up to the dais and sit on the arm of his chair picturing in my mind the ludicrous aspect of this scene —a huge black ventriloquist with a 48-year-old white dummy on his lap. Ali is going into gory detail about how I had to shoot his hands before every fight, a fact I do not necessarily want publicized for obvious reasons. He finally winds down and thanks me for past services, and I say, "And thank *you*, Champ, for blowing my license in every state in the union."

This gets a laugh and I am off, except that Ali seems appalled that he did anything that could possibly hurt me, and he tries to straighten it out with a typical other-foot-in-the-mouth remark. "This doctor is world famous. That's my doctor, Dr. Pacheco, a well-known *Chicago* doctor."

That afternoon at five we have a private screening of a fight film called *Rocky*. I see an old friend from *Sports Illustrated*, Mort Sharnik, and discuss some piece I have written for SI at length, and as we finish talking the first images appear on the screen. It is a scene straight out of a Bellows painting. The picture gets better and better. It turns out to be the strongest boxing movie since Budd Schulberg's *The Harder They Fall*. The picture is over in what seems to be too short a time, and I find myself on my feet applauding. Emotionally drained, I leave the studio on cloud nine.

Back at the hotel I begin to get ready to go to Bob Arum's party at his apartment. I have told Petula, Budd Schulberg, and Norman Lear I will meet them there, but the phone rings and I am short-circuited. My dearest friend in Europe, Jarvis Astaire, is calling to remind me that I am to go to the opening of *Marathon Man,* with Dustin Hoffman, and on to a dinner afterward at 21. I had never received this message, but when Jarvis calls I go with him. We always see each other when he is in town or I am in London.

Marathon Man is playing on Times Square to a preview audience and the theatre is packed. Jarvis introduces me to his London chums, Mr. and Mrs. John Gold, and a New York insurance broker, Neal Walsh, and his beautiful blonde wife. All of the ladies are dressed in high-fashion black; she is dressed in all white. Why do I mention that? She is beautiful.

Hours before I stood and applauded a small sleeper movie *Rocky;* now I slink out of the theatre to scattered boos and hisses. *Marathon Man* may make a lot more money than *Rocky,* but there is no comparison in the quality of the work. (Later—the critics at least thought so too. *Rocky* was voted best picture of the year.)

Jarvis manages to capture his feeling of the worth of the film in a brief understatement to his London chum. "I think we had better rule out this film as the chosen one for the Royal Premiere."

His loyalty to the Queen overshadows his loyalty to his client Dustin Hoffman. He may be Hoffman's manager, but he is a Loyal Servant of the Royal Family first. His obligation to protect the Queen's sensibilities is greater than his obligation to fatten his client's pocketbook. A wise choice, I'm sure, since there is more violence and killing in this film than there was at Verdun.

After the dismal premiere we repair to 21 to lick our wounds: here the usual jockeying for the *right table* goes on, providing New York psychiatrists with a waiting line of patients who take such things seriously. It is always amazing to me that captains of industry and stars can be brought crashing down to earth in a quivering hulk of anxieties by being seated at a "bad" table by a frozen-faced head waiter. I often have the feeling that the maître d's are really psychiatrists in disguise drumming up business. But Jarvis gets the "right" table so it does not seem to be his problem of the moment.

At the TV viewing room I spot Mike Burke, the genial head of Madison Square Garden, watching the Redskins win an overtime game with the hapless Eagles. He is telling his guest, John Ringling North, that the fight should pull in forty thousand people. The old showman clucks appreciatively but his eyes mirror disbelief. A weary Cosell is telling his late viewers that he is catching a red-eye flight home, and a distant voice behind him says "So what?", which seems just the right note with which to leave for Arum's party.

Bob Arum has invited just a "few" inside people to his apartment, but there turns out to be an awful lot of inside people in New York, and the place is overflowing.

I missed the main event, which almost invariably involves Norman Mailer. There is an aura of violence on the night before a fight that affects combative people, and it always seems to surface in Norman who, as the years pass, seems less able to carry out his self-destructive desires. This night I hear he zeroes in on Budd Schulberg who has been described as a sweet bear of a man. This longstanding on-and-off main event has been smoldering for years and is usually forestalled by Budd Schulberg's wife, who is as sensible as she is beautiful. When she spots Norman in the same room with Budd, with the old fire coming out of his nostrils, she quietly but firmly leads Budd out of harm's way.

Unfortunately this night Geraldine is in Hollywood shooting a picture and Budd is prowling Manhattan on his own, ready to talk fights and fighting in his knowledgeable way, and ready to back his opinion physically if needed. Inexorably Mailer and Schulberg gravitate to a central location, where the verbiage heats up and both begin to square off, or belly up since both are now distinctively middle-aged and not in combat condition. Ironically, both these authors are the top authorities on fights and boxing in this century, and both are antagonistic to each other for reasons best known to themselves.

As the threats and insults fly, Mailer butts Schulberg's head. "Foul. Foul! He butted me!" cries Schulberg, and they are separated, each to retreat to his corner comforted by friends and literary groupies. Thus another big confrontation fizzles out with a poof, and the party breaks up, each man going his separate way ready to resume the hostilities at the next heavyweight championship fight, which may be in another three years or so. Plenty of time to train for that one.

SEPTEMBER 28—TUESDAY

I wake with a sense of extreme excitement. Fight day at last! Time to get it on and time to get it over with. I dress hurriedly and go to Ali's suite at the Essex. He has arrived from Harold Conrad's apartment and is dressed in his customary black pants and shirt, sipping a little juice. Then he gets up and takes off his clothes, and sits on the sofa in his terrycloth robe.

Ali is half listening to Cus D'Amato, the old fight manager and trainer of Floyd Patterson. Ali has spotted him in the lobby and had him come up to his suite. Cus is pouring on the advice and Ali is nodding. All the things Cus is saying are true and Ali nods solemnly as if he is hearing this advice for the first time. Suddenly he gets the old Ali mischievous little-kid grin, and I know he has an idea cooking.

Cus is now partially deaf and he looks like an old Mister Magoo with squinty eyes and pursed lips, his hand to his good ear cupped to catch the sounds as best he can. In the corner is Lloyd Wells, deaf in one ear from an old football injury and getting deaf in the other. Ali signals to Angelo to pretend to talk to him, but not to make a sound. Bingham, the photographer, and I are called in and we are pantomiming a conversation in a rerun of the oldest gag. Cus leans forward trying to read the lips of Ali through his squinty eyes. Lloyd, for whom the gag is not intended, looks confused. After five minutes of this Ali turns to Cus and whispers a question. Cus catches it and whispers back. This breaks up Ali and they all have a good laugh over the childish gag. Over in the corner chair Lloyd slumps back and says, more to himself than to anyone in the room, "Thank god! I thought the left ear had gone on me."

The doorbell rings, and in the absence of Pat Patterson I answer. There stands a little man in sneakers with a liniment bottle in his hand and a towel over his shoulder.

"I'm sorry, we already have a masseur for Ali," I say, but he skitters by into the dressing room. A few moments later Harold Conrad comes by and takes me into the dressing room and I am amazed to see Mara Conrad flat on her stomach on the floor with the masseur walking on her back, his sneakers still on, leaving suction cup marks on her back. Mara suffers from the dancer's curse, a bad back, and I cannot think that this is anything more unusual than what always happens in a heavyweight champion's dressing room before a weigh-in. At least, in *this* champion's rooms.

A while later, Jeremiah Shabazz comes with the news that we are wanted for the weigh-in. Norton has come and gone. John X. is finally getting wise to the impracticability of having the two boxers on stage at the same time.

In the hall the advance guard of the Faithful Fifty are waiting and we avalanche into the elevator.

The Empire Room is packed with press and visitors. Ali weighs in at 220 and starts to speak. The crowd hushes expectantly and Ali does a fast half hour. He spots Dustin Hoffman in the crowd with his manager, Jarvis Astaire, and calls them up to the mike.

"*My main man, Dustin Hoffman,*" Ali yells in mock excitement, towering over the diminutive actor. "Who you for tonight?"

Dustin, who is a friend of both Norton and Ali, squirms uneasily under Ali's glare and neatly sidesteps. "I'd rather vote for you than either Carter *or* Ford," Dustin says, and exits laughing.

In the audience the ticket shuffle goes on. Blackie Lisker, sports editor of the *Star,* comes up offering a contract for one super good ticket for his boss' wife, Lady Murdoch, but I have just given my last two-hundred-buck seat to Norman Lear who needs it for the president of CBS, who responds gracefully by accepting the ticket, then not showing up at the fight. Poor Lady Murdoch, I wonder where she saw the fight. I wonder if Blackie still has a job. I know Norman Lear has.

The weigh-in safely over, Ali retreats to his hideaway and Angelo and I decide to go to Yankee Stadium to check the ring, a ritual that Angelo does that has saved many a fight for his fighters. Dr. Gordon decides to accompany us. So does Jimmy Dundee, Angelo's son. So does Lowell Riley, Herbert's man and photographer, and Tony, another of the same breed. We are loaded down with tinware and photographic equipment as we head for the Stadium. Before we go, we eat at a delicatessen that has smashingly good hot dogs and run across Harold Valen, the referee, who might work the fight tonight. He handled a controversial decision when Angelo had Jimmy Ellis fighting Patterson in Stockholm and has been semiostracized since. He is a nice man and we all hope he gets the call, but it is not to be.

Outside, the first load catches a cab and Angelo and I wait for the next cab, only to find ourselves standing next to the never-stop funny man Henny Youngman, who is a fight nut. He greets us and hands me a piece of folded paper. "Here's a note for you, Doc."

I open the note to find a blank piece of paper with a large musical note painted on it. I laugh helplessly. I am Henny's fool. Now he hails a cab, and as it pulls up he sticks his head in the door and says to the cab driver, "Sorry, I am off duty."

Henny turns and walks away and we take the cab. The driver is not laughing. End of a two-joke Youngman monologue.

Yankee Stadium is aswarm with workmen. We hit a gate and are met by a competent Madison Square Garden man who takes us around to show us the dressing rooms, the way we are going to enter the ring, and so forth. He is all business and sounds like John X. in the detailed way he had all the security planned and pathways blocked and passes given out. I say innocently, "Maybe this is going to work out the same wonderful way it does in the Garden."

"What do you mean? The Garden takes care of national conventions and bigger shows than this. We do it all at the Garden."

Poor man, what use is it to tell him that his well-laid plans will come to naught when the Faithful Fifty come hurtling down the aisle? At the time this man was sure he had it all laid out perfectly. The last anyone saw of him, he was being carried out on the shoulders of a mob of teenage werewolves who invaded the areas that only people with special passes and green wrist bands were supposed to be in. I meant to talk to him after the fight but I didn't have the heart.

Back in the city I drive with Dr. Gordon to the Waldorf to give Petula a vitamin shot before her opening. I meet Claude, her husband, in the lobby and he is unrecognizable in a beard, although it looks good on him. He looks like a French-Jewish privateer. Those were the kind that didn't take a boat by force but took it in a proxy fight.

"Petula is just about through with the rehearsal—can you wait a moment?" I say yes and sit in a darkened room to hear Petula finish her rehearsal. As I sit down I recognize the closing chorus of "Downtown" which Petula opens the show with, which means, in a dress rehearsal, I will have to sit through the whole show before I can give her the shot. I must say that I never mind hearing a whole Petula Clark show, and I enjoy this long rest from the prefight tenseness. Petula is finally through and I administer her medication. We kiss good luck and go off in separate directions to fight our respective fights. She won hers by a KO opening night. We, on the other hand, did not do quite as well.

Back at the hotel I am in time to pick up my fight stuff and pack my friends in a limo that Buddy Howe has thoughtfully provided for the evening. Had he known the kind of evening he was headed for he might have provided an armored car.

Zev Bufman, the Israeli-American dynamo theatrical promoter, has brought his beautiful wife Velma to the fights although she hates violence and eats vegetables to prove it. He is a welcome addition to the group, which includes the Gordons, Luisita, and Buddy Howe. They proceed to Sardi's for supper, and I take off to the Essex where I grab a cold cup of coffee in Angelo's room, which is brimming to overflow with family and friends. I eat half of Vicky La Motta's cupcake and talk to her about the upcoming film on her ex-husband, Jake La Motta, the Bronx Bull, to be played by Robert DeNiro. He is the best actor around today, but slight and definitely *not* a boxer type of the grim destroyer kind that Jake was in his prime. Leaving that to smarter people than I, we gather up our gear and Sarria, the silent Cuban, and I head downstairs with Bundini and Youngblood (Wali). At the door there wait nine limos laid on for the workers and crew.

True to form, the nine limos are either gone or overflowing with the Faithful Fifty and their ladies and families. Angelo waves down a cab and we all pile in. The Puerto Rican driver objects to Wali's son coming in with us, although the lad is a slight teenager. The scene is nasty and gets uglier until the kid hooks a ride in a limo. We drive in smoldering anger through Harlem. It is strangely quiet, the silence being broken only by the faroff wail of an ambulance racing to the scene of another fight whose results are more clear cut than the one we are headed for will be. The cab driver pulls up and as we exit asks for a ticket to the fight. Wali's answer is a classic, but unprintable.

Yankee Stadium is lit up and the scene is pandemonium. The cops are on strike and marching. The kids, seeing that they will not be molested by law and order that night, are organizing into frenzied bands inclined to mayhem. The film *Clockwork Orange* comes to mind. The streets belong to the mob. People are getting robbed within touching distance of the gates, and the cops are watching. They will not come out of the safety of Yankee Stadium. I do not blame them. They do not have green wrist bands that will permit them to get back in. This is being run with *Madison Square Garden* efficiency.

Our hardy band tries to get in the press gate. Hands massage my pockets, pull at my coat, try to wrest my doctor's bag from my hands. I am in a fight like none I have ever experienced. What is the delay? Where is the holdup? Why isn't Sarria moving?

At the turnstile a ticket taker is checking each ticket and questioning the owners. Obviously we have all the identifying tickets and the bands are all the right colors, but we are stymied by those ahead and have nowhere to go. Breathing gets difficult. Poor Sarria is getting his flat feet stepped on and his face is contorted in pain. Bundini is yelling but it serves no purpose, as slowly we are being pushed through the gate by the mob. The effect is like being pushed through the neck of a bottle. But once you pop through and are inside, no one is around you and that produces a most gratifying effect. Our band regroups, ready to find our dressing room and fix it for the champ's arrival. Our super-efficient Madison Square Garden guide from this afternoon cusses as he leads us through a dugout to our dressing room. He does not appear as confident as he did this afternoon.

We enter a dressing room which I presume is the Yankee dressing room since it is spacious and rather lavish. Each of us goes about preparing his stuff for the fight. The night is cold and I am wearing a black Ali sweatshirt under my white doctor's smock that has MUHAMMAD ALI emblazoned on the back in giant red letters. Once I wore this to the hospital and office without realizing it until late afternoon, when my nurse mentioned I had Muhammad Ali written all over my shirt. Don't I always, I asked?

Outside, at ringside, the celebrities are gathering. The air is not as charged as at the first Ali-Frazier fight, but then I don't think any fight will achieve that electric high again. I see Jean-Paul Belmondo, quietly sitting, unobserved and unnoticed by a New York crowd more interested in the old champion Joe Louis and the old Yankee hero Joe Di Maggio, once again an instantly recognizable figure because of his bank commercials. Telly Savalas sweeps in with a mini-entourage. Don Sutherland has sprouted a huge beard and is almost unrecognizable. Joe Barcelona, mysterious new power man from Newark, is in a front row seat with a bodyguard next to him. Barry White and his pregnant and imposing wife Cleopatra have a haggard look from fighting their way through the mob. They *are* recognizable and the mob has virtually torn Barry's coat off. It is a taste of things to come.

Forty-five minutes before the fight, Ali comes in. He is calm but his followers are excited. Kilroy says the car could not get through the mob to get close to the gate. Bingham, that excellent photographer, is so excited he is no longer stuttering. The crowd had spotted the Ali limo and mobbed it, jumping on the fenders and hood until it could not proceed further. Ali wisely decided not to get out and walk since a mob like that has the love that kills. The limo edged through the crowd and into the Stadium.

Ali dresses in his fight gear. Wali lovingly lays out each item of apparel and Bundini and Angelo are watching every move. Next to them Jeremiah is trying to sort out the crowd that has made their way into our dressing room. In spite of the elaborate system of checks and precautions, the room is rapidly filling up with the Faithful Fifty. This group can infiltrate better than Viet Cong guerillas. The camera crews start to set up for the required dressing-room footage. I have an opportunity to talk to an old Miami acquaintance, Bob Halloran, who is now doing a great job in New York as a sportscaster. He is one of the few to start out with Ali at the beginning, and he doesn't show any signs of aging during the past ten years.

Budd Schulberg appears, showing no scars from losing his fight on a butt, but not asking for a rematch either. The gimmick man is in a corner putting his gold Ali pendants on the cornermen and anyone else who will sit still. Ed Hughes, the ex-barber, is limping around on his bad leg, aggravated by the cold, complaining about the adverse effects of the cold weather and the location of his seat. Jimmy Ellis, the former champion, is quietly sitting in a corner and looking worried for Ali, and relieved that he no longer has to suffer this terrible prefight tension.

Time is short. Ali has his little daughter on his lap now, kissing her, while a slick, well-turned-out uptown dude glides in and says some appropriate complimentary remarks to the little girl. Ali regards the pimp icily. "Hitting on this girl already? Man, get out of here with your jive, your kind ain't ever gonna be around my little girl."

He hugs his gorgeous daughter and she beams a radiant smile. The pimp slinks out, confused, but still happy to have contact with Ali. General Custer enters and takes up his place by Ali. General Custer who idolizes Ali and comes to every fight, invited by Ali, is the white manager of rock star Wayne Cochran. He is one of the few white members of the Faithful Fifty. He has a huge head of blondish hair and a mustache and goatee like General Custer wore.

Ali is not warming up and we are ten minutes away from getting in the ring. For an athlete of his or any age not to warm up on a cold night is a cardinal sin in boxing, but Ali has decided to save up his energy for the fight. He will need it. His usually glistening butter-brown skin is ashy and has a whitish tint. Lloyd Wells points this out and tells Ali to put vaseline on his legs so that they won't look like he has "the whites." Ali disdains the advice and does a little TV interview, while behind him the more agile of the Faithful Fifty angle for camera exposure.

Time is out; the signal to go in has come from the Garden people. Jeremiah gathers the Faithful Fifty and gives them stern instructions. "You all have your tickets for seats. Go out now and get seated. Don't try to come in the ring with us because only the workers are going in with us. OK. Each of you go to your seats."

Each member nods vigorously and looks at the man next to him. "Right. You heard the man. Just the workers go in. You guys go on out to your seats."

No one moves and the harried man from the Garden gives the signal to Murray Goodman, who gives us the signal, and we move forward as one. Angelo, Wali, Sarria, and I, wise to the crunch, hustle ahead to try to get in the ring first. We are unmolested as we move into it. John X. has said that only the four corner workers will be allowed in the ring and press section. The rest of the Faithful Fifty will have to sit in their seats. I look up as I ascend the ring stairs to see Kilroy holding open the ropes with Lloyd Wells. In the aisle at ringside I see the rest of the Faithful Fifty infiltrating the press section, and down the aisle I see Ali about to be swept up into the ring by his hysterical followers. He seems unruffled. In the other corner I see only a grimly determined Norton with his three men and Bobby Goodman, the ace publicity man in charge of the arrangements, leaving the ring. What a contrast.

Ali is in the ring now, circling and looking at Norton. He does his show biz turn and says a few taunting things to Norton, and Norton fixes him with a flinty stare. After twenty-four rounds of fighting Ali, Norton is not to be intimidated. He looks ready and his beautifully muscled body is glistening with sweat under the lights. He *has* warmed up.

Introductions are over and Ali returns to receive his mouthpiece and remove his robe. He turns in silent prayer with Wali, and down below in the press section Herbert Muhammad bows his head. Reflexively, Chris Dundee, sitting next to Herbert, bows his head as well. I would guess we all said a silent prayer this night.

Round one, and Ali is jabbing fast and moving well. It figures to be Ali's round as he sets a fast pace. He returns to the corner and stands up, not sitting down for a quick rest. I look over at Norton and he is doing the same. No way to psych this Norton. *Round two,* and Norton gets brave and puts some things together. Ali returns calmly to the corner. We all think he has won both rounds but the official scorecards show that he has lost round two. Inexplicably he goes to the rope-a-dope trick for rounds three and four and takes a good rib pounding by Norton, but he returns unruffled to the corner. Now we have the fight even. He goes out to win round five, and so he does, but he is looking very slow. He is not fast of hand and his punches seem to have an amateurish quality when compared to the Ali of just one year ago. He is not tired, but looks inexplicably weary of the whole thing. He is not "fighting happy." There is no joy in his fight; he is doing the things mechanically that he usually does, but *sin brio*. He continues to stand in the corner, refusing water or any restoring help from the cornermen. He does not want to be rubbed. He does not want to be touched. His conversation is limited to one question as he returns to the corner: "Who won that round?" A cacophony of advice comes from four mouths but he seems not to hear. He listens mainly to the main man and brains of the corner, Angelo Dundee, but he does not accept advice easily at this stage of his career and still goes out and does what comes into his handsome head. Ali, at this stage, cannot be told anything, which can be dangerous in the tough game of boxing.

The middle rounds have drifted by in the same seesaw pattern and Ali appears to be sleepwalking through the fight. A shadow of Ali is in with Norton, but Norton is 100 percent there. Still the shadow is able to hold even, and at times summons up energy from a hidden reservoir and shows some of the splendor of the old Ali fighting machine. Norton is swinging savagely but mostly missing, as the films will later show. Ali is flicking but landing punches seemingly without steam. He returns to stand again in the corner. His gigantic pride will not allow his aching body to sit down and admit his age and weariness. In the other corner Norton stands too. Toward the end of the first ten rounds, something snaps the old Ali back on and he dances for a round, popping a confused Norton at will. The old Ali of Houston, Miami, and Maine fame would have eaten Norton alive by now but Norton, fighting the shadow of greatness past, is holding his own. The final five start, and in the eleventh round Norton catches Ali with a sweeping hook to the rib cage. Ali winces and bends over in pain. I look at Angelo. He might have a broken rib, we both think. I look back at Herbert who will have to be the one to stop it if it comes to that, and his head is buried in his hands. He has been in deep prayer since the fifth round. He genuinely loves Ali and does not want to see him hurt or floundering around like an echo of his former self. Ali comes back to the corner again, and says the punch hurt but the rib does not hurt at this point. I press it with a great deal of force, but get no reaction. No fractured rib. Back to the fray. At this point the corner feels Ali is behind and must win the remaining rounds. He does win most of the rest of the rounds, but by the bell that opens round fifteen we are all in accord that the fight is even. We need the fifteenth round to win. It has come back to that once again. Can Ali pull it out once again with that gigantic champion's heart? Can he find the way to win? Ali is old and tired but his will to win is the same as when he stepped into his first amateur fight, and he is truly an exceptional champion and an exceptional human being. I look over at Norton who is snorting fire. Rahaman, Ali's younger brother, has been making regular trips to the corner to exhort Ali to win and to wake him up, but Ali regards him kindly and tells him to go sit down. Angelo is working well now, earning his money. He is telling Ali what he already knows. We win this round or goodbye title. Ali turns, takes a big breath, and goes out to meet Norton who comes racing across the ring. Ali dances and pops and Norton follows like a raging bull, but his punches are not landing and he is being frustrated while Ali is pecking away with light punches that are landing. Angelo is screaming "Fight him, fight him, goddamn you, fight him!" but Ali knows what his weary body can take and he is drifting through a haze of exhaustion to win the round on points on all three scorecards.

The fight ends and Ali returns to the corner. Still he refuses to sit down. We all disobey the cardinal axiom of boxing. When a close fight is over, *look like a winner*. The cornermen and the fighter should jump around in glee so that, if a close unpopular decision goes for us, it does not look as bad. Instead we all look depressed, including Ali, who has his head bowed in an uncharacteristic pose. His nose is dripping blood and looks broken, his ribs ache, his hands hurt, and he is very tired.

The announcer reads the cards which give Ali a close split decision and there is an unearthly lack of sound from the crowd. They don't boo, but they don't cheer.

The press seems evenly divided, and the ring begins to fill with the masses that are getting by the efficient Garden cordon of security. Everywhere I turn I meet the eyes of newsmen I know and they all seem mildly apologetic. So do I. Have we all witnessed that night we have been dreading? The night that Ali is no longer Ali, but just another fighter? Off this fight, it appears so.

Ali leaves hurriedly, followed by an unusually silent mass of followers. I wait to catch a glimpse of Luisita, for the ringside has turned into an unruly mob scene. Young thugs have raced up the aisles snatching purses, flinging themselves into the ring. The police and the efficient Garden people seem powerless to stop them. The first two rows of ringside seats are overturned. A lady snaps her leg and goes down hard. In the front seat, Helen Dundee and her mother are fighting hard to remain upright, and when it is over Helen is left in uncontrollable hysteria, shaking and almost convulsive. Around ringside the patrons gather together in protective clumps, like people on the stern of the sinking *Titanic*. Luisita, wise in the ways of the Ali postfight scenes, has taken off to the rear. Buddy Howe, Lear, and the group escape to attempt to find their waiting limo. On hitting the street they find the mob scene more violent and menacing than in the Stadium, so they escape to Nedick's. On entering, Buddy is double-teamed by the old drop-your-change routine, wherein one guy drops his change, bends over to pick it up, and the other confederate behind him pushes the victim over him to be rolled. Unfortunately for them, Buddy Howe has been a professional acrobat for many years and retains his keen sense of balance. On this occasion he pushes the front man over and elbows the back man over as well, deftly skipping over the confused mass of struggling humanity to the relative safety of the Nedick's counter.

I have also broken my cardinal rule of survival. I always head for the dressing room *before* Ali comes in. After all, it's a time when my services are often needed most. But in looking out for Luisita and the party, I am caught outside the dressing room with Ali inside. It takes me a full half hour to fight through the hangers-on and newsmen waiting outside Ali's door. I am crushed from front and back. My arms are weary from holding my medical bag aloft and it gets worse as I approach the door, for the push is truly breathtaking here. Strange that the efficient Garden people, with all of their experience in national conventions and big events, could not control the dressing-room tunnels, which have only one small entrance, to guard against people not wearing green wrist bands.

Once inside I enter a different world. The screaming and panic are behind and I enter the atmosphere of a funeral parlor. Ali is laid out in the other room, and a few of the hardies who have made it this far are hanging around the interview table within camera range. I enter the other room to examine Ali's nose and rib.

Ali is strangely and completely quiet. He is exhausted as I go through the necessary examination. He does not wince or cry out. He is stoic. The nose *looks* broken but the examination does not reveal it. We will have to wait for X-rays, but not tonight. Quietly he speaks to me. "I don't have it any more. I was not myself out there. I see the things to do but I can't do them. Did I win the fight? Am I through, Doc? Should I quit?" Then, as if answering his own questions, he continues, "I think I will hang them up. I think I am through. What do you think?"

"I wish you would quit now. I would be the happiest person of your entourage if you quit now, but I don't think you will."

"Yes, I will." Then silence, and after a few moments, "But you know, Doc, I can knock out Foreman every time I fight him. Norton will always be hard for me. I can't hit him good but Foreman is a chump and I am his Daddy. He cannot get out of the way of my punches. I can beat that sucker every time out."

I look at this exhausted warrior. His body has died, but his spirit is still the same spirit of the 18-year-old Cassius Clay. Maybe he is right, maybe he can knock out George Foreman, but is the risk of real injury worth it? Is it worth ten million?

I am not involved in his financial world, only in his physical world, and I would not like to see anything happen to this exceptional human being. So I pat him on the back, make him comfortable, and fade away, knowing that if he chooses to fight again I will respond to his call like the sappiest member of the Faithful Fifty because, for whatever disparate reasons, we all have one thing in common: we all love this guy.

By now it is close to one-thirty in the morning. The crews are cleaning up Yankee Stadium and my people have left. I go by Kenny's dressing room to offer sincere condolences. Bobby Goodman is handling his dressing room and there is no one left but a newsman taping an interview. His manager tells Norton that I am outside and he winds up the interview as I stand there. He is still close to tears. I shrug and offer my hand. "It was a helluva fight, Kenny, and after three fights I still don't know who won any of them. If it's any consolation to you, I think you retired him."

"If he retires, I retire. I don't want no other fight but Ali again."

"Kenny, stay in the game, and pick up the big money. That is the name of the fight game."

"Thanks, Doc, I'll see you around."

He gives me his million-dollar smile and we shake hands. I hope I never have to look at Ken Norton's face across the ring again from Ali's corner. He is one tough nut for Ali.

I drift outside to look for a ride and run into Sally Gries waiting for Tom to pack up his camera crew and equipment. She innocently wants to go out to the street to catch a cab. She is tall, beautiful, blonde, buxom, and with diamond rings and a fur coat on. I convince her that sanity must make her wait for Tom and the crew.

By two Tom is ready, and we have the poor sense of timing to run out at the same time as some of Ali's group come out, so we attract the howling minions. Again we have to fight our way to the street, but fortuitously a cab comes out of nowhere and we leave the scene of rioting to break all existing street speed records to the Warwick. To cap off the evening, we get a junkie cab driver with a heavy foot. We careen down empty streets taking every corner on two wheels. In the front seat, Tom Shaw clings to a knob on the dash and is gritting his teeth while regarding the madman through bulging eyeballs.

We arrive at the Warwick where our haggard family awaits. We troop the one block to the Stage Delicatessen and get in under the wire. The place is buzzing with fight talk but I merely listen to the riot and horror stories of the people around me.

Mort Sharnik of *Sports Illustrated* has lost his wallet. An English newsman has been hit over the head and robbed. A man has been stabbed at the gate and another was stripped and robbed within view of the ticket taker, then refused admission because he did not have a ticket. Marge Cowan, owner of the Diplomat in Miami Beach, has lost her pocketbook and all her jewels. Joe Barcelona, the new Newark power, has lost his expensive wristwatch. The stories are painfully similar. It was the night that Ali stepped into the past and New York City stepped into the future.

13·Fight Doctor

The main difficulty I have had as Ali's doctor has been to keep all the assorted medical types that hang around a fighter from adding their two bits. Now let me get this straight lest my medical colleagues begin to get their lawsuits prepared. By medical types I mean *all* types of people that have to do with the health of an athlete, which includes masseurs, chiropractors, osteopaths, dental hygienists, bunion pad salesmen, medical writers, TV interviewers, gym doctors, pimps, hustlers, and numbers men from Cleveland. See what I mean?

Muhammad Ali has been blessed by the greatest body God could create. He is the next thing to the Six Million Dollar Man, and in some ways better. He does not have to sweat out the ratings to see if his act will be renewed for next year. My whole concept as a boxer's doctor is to do as little as possible to prepare a fighter for a fight, as little as possible to patch him up during the fight, and patch him up as simply as possible after a fight. Overtreatment has ruined many a great potential fighter. Let me explain.

A fighter is usually a young man in the prime of life, with an innate toughness of mind and body. A weak body does not last long in this environment, and it's unlikely one will ever even start out in it. So the fighter arrives fresh and ready to do what is needed to get himself ready for combat. If he is fortunate, he falls in the hands of a great trainer, like Angelo Dundee, or Gil Clancey, or Luis Sarria, or many of the true boxing men of earlier days. But soon some older fighters begin to talk to him. Younger fighters are very gullible. They look for crutches. They hear that so-and-so always drinks a gallon of sugar-laden orange juice, some guy takes this shot, the other smokes a joint before a fight, still another uses this drug or that or eats a certain thing. They listen to stories containing a variety of crutches and substitutes for the real thing: *hard work and conditioning.*

The first thing I tell these young men is that there is no substitute for roadwork, gym work, proper dieting, and proper rest. You noticed that I didn't mention sex. Sex was a tremendous bugaboo in the old days of boxing, when the world was much more naïve, with sexual mores and attitudes enmeshed in antiquated old wives' tales, suspicions, and ignorances. Nat Fleischer, the old authority on boxing, writing in his book on *Training Fighters,* starts his chapter on masturbation with the priceless sentence: "Masturbation is the scourge of Western Man." He had no section on oral sex, a thought so abhorrent to him that he did not consider any effect it might have on fighters, since he refused to recognize that it existed. It is no wonder that until a few fighters like Muhammad Ali disproved the antiquated trainers' hypothesis, all trainers held that an orgasm before a fight was worse than a blow to the area in question. Like many of the old boxing gym axioms, sexual abstinence is good but for the wrong reasons.

Sexual experiences cannot be considered as isolated phenomena, and this alone furnishes boxing trainers with one good reason to support their position. In order to have a sexual experience you should have a partner. In order to get a partner one has to do some serious, time-consuming, mind-distracting work. Point one: Seduction is very time consuming and distracting. There is an old, wise boxing trainer named Bill Gore who, in the days when black people tried to be white by emulating their appearance, would say, "Show me a black guy that straightens his hair and I'll show you a fighter ready to be taken!" *Translation:* As soon as a guy gets into the business of looking good, and chasing around after girls in expensive joints, his mind is off fighting, and you have lost a fighter.

Old fight people are firm in the belief that an orgasm is highly weakening. One timely story springs to mind to illustrate this point. Willie Pastrano was a great, lightning-fast light-heavyweight who won the championship late in his boxing life. He claimed that he had to have some sexual adventure every day or he would have a headache. Willie had not had a headache since he was 10 years old. Angelo, tired of bird-dogging him, assigned an old trainer named Lou Gross to watch Willie while he trained in the Catskills for his fight with Jose Torres.

Willie would train and then retire to his room, ostensibly to take a nap; however, Willie had done his search, seek, and seduce mission, and had ladies who would accompany him to tuck him into bed. Lou Gross was busy in the lobby watching out for hookers, widows, and showgirls while Willie was upstairs brightening the day for the enitre staff of the hotel. Owners of the hotel were amazed at the sprightly, happy attitude of their female employees, and attributed it to better vacuum cleaners and a lighter workload.

One afternoon, a disgruntled girl took Lou Gross aside and informed him of what was happening in Willie's room at the moment. Lou stared at her in disbelief, as if she was suggesting that Willie had just contracted cholera. Dashing upstairs, he took out the key to Willie's room, opened the door, and stared in horrified disbelief. There was the title about to be given away by one impending orgasm. Quickly the axioms of Nat Fleischer came to mind, and he sprang into the room shouting at top voice, *"Don't come, Willie!!! Don't come!!!"*

A bewildered Willie recalled he had one of the greatest headaches of his young life that afternoon. To this day Lou Gross imputes the massacre of Willie by Torres in the Garden, and the loss of the title, to Willie's loose morals and profligate, extravagant womanizing. Torres attributes it to a devastating body attack. So does Pastrano.

Willie was a wag, a gym lawyer, and a doctor practicing without a license. Young fighters would listen to his theories, and those foolish enough to accompany him on his afternoon rounds of socializing usually paid for it in the ring. A sign appeared in the gym stating: IS AN HOUR OF FUN WORTH A LIFETIME OF GUILT? Willie wrote in large red pencil: HOW DO YOU MAKE IT LAST AN HOUR?

Willie, like many an old intelligent pro, got by with what would kill most young fighters. One reason was his brilliant defensive style of fighting. The other was his genuine desire to stay in one piece, which fueled his considerable defensive engine, enabling him to run and flick his jab at a faster and faster rate than normally is seen in the ring. *But Willie was the exception to the rule.*

If I have strayed from the point let me make it. Sexual activity is not, per se, bad for a fighter. But it is possible that sexual abstinence before a fight is good for him, because it stokes up his emotional furnace. That is to say, sex deprivation makes a man in his prime testy. Aggression is built up after prolonged sexual deprivation. If you do not believe this, read the history of Western Civilization. If a man is mean and mad and resentful and angry, he is known in the fight game as having a good edge. He is ready for a fight. Therefore, sexual abstinence six weeks before a fight should make a man ready to kill, and so the old savants in the gyms may have been right to withhold sexual relief from their tigers, even if for the wrong reasons.

The rest of the crutches can be dispensed with by the same simple approach I mentioned previously: *There is no substitute for proper roadwork, gym work, diet, and rest.*

Still, a fighter may come to the office for "help" before a fight, and sometimes, if I feel he will be aided in the same way I aid a hypochondriac, I will give him a vitamin shot, which goes straight through him and into the toilet. He feels he has an edge, but if he did not do his work, he is in for a long evening. And sometimes this approach backfires.

Al Jones was a huge six-foot-five-inch black fighter we were developing, and he was building up a considerable knockout record on Miami Beach. This night he was to fight an old sparring partner named Willie Johnson, who was a disciple of the Willie Pastrano *never-had-a-headache school.* Now I worked with both fighters, but I was going to be in Al Jones' corner for this one. Johnson came to my office the morning of the fight with a doleful look in his eye. He had been weak the night before and had fallen prey to a seductive sister of the street, and he was in my office for me to rectify this momentary failing with a huge restoring shot of the magic stuff I gave Pastrano. Willie had told Johnson that I had magic in a syringe to perk him up. Feeling sorry for the fallen one, and knowing the king-sized beating that probably awaited him that night, I gave him a vitamin injection, but warned him that it would not infuse him with a talent that was not his to begin with.

He nodded and bounded off happily to the thrashing that awaited him across the bay. Willie was knocked out in four, and had the colossal nerve to state to the boxing commission and newspapers that he was drugged.

Getting back to Ali, you can now appreciate that, aside from taking care of the acute medical problems, my other main preoccupation has been to fend off the assorted quacks and characters who offer Ali these panaceas and artificial aids. But to his credit, although Ali has an ingratiating habit of appearing to listen to *anyone* that comes up with an idea, and *appearing* to do what he suggests, he seldom carries through on what is suggested and thereby saves himself from disaster.

The early Ali, the young Cassius Clay, had no medical difficulties. His young body was a marvelous machine that needed few ministrations. The years of exile when he was stripped of his title eroded his finely tuned machine, because for the first time in his career he permitted himself full liberties which he had always denied himself. In addition to dietary excesses, he got married and divorced and came upon a proverb of his generation: *You don't have to be married to go to bed with a girl.* So in the three years of exile Ali made up for lost time. In his words, he was *dancing,* and his dance was the horizontal rumba.

When it became a fact that we were going to return to the boxing world via the Jerry Quarry fight in Atlanta, Georgia, Ali had to go back into serious training, but now it was oh so much harder, and one of the harder things to do without were the foxes that kept coming out of the woods to chase the magnificent Ali. There wasn't much of a chase to catch Ali.

In the Fifth Street Gym where he was training, the crowds would gather and most of them were foxes to look at and admire. One afternoon I brought over my two friends Claude Wolff and his wife, Petula Clark, both dyed-in-the-wool fight fans. Ali, who recognizes famous faces but cannot often come up with names, looked over the ring ropes at the cute Petula and went into his sparring act, which that day consisted of letting his sparring partner pound on his midsection.

In this case the sparring partner was Alvin (Blue) Lewis, a huge black man from Detroit who can punch with authority.

In the midst of this exhibition, Ali doubled over and went down, making a big joke out of the whole thing, but stopping the sparring right then. The clowning covered up the hurt and we retired to the cubicle where Sarria usually rubbed away his hurts. Suddenly the fight seemed endangered, and things began to look bleak. Ali shook it off and did not want X-rays taken. By nightfall I began to get worried calls from his men. In the morning I talked to Herbert and agreed to X-ray Ali in my office and have a close-mouthed, discreet radiologist named Carlos Llanes read the film. The rib appeared questionable, a thin hairline fracture barely visible, and a possible separation of the cartilage from the bone. Things were looking worse.

Ali, as usual, took it better than all of us and said to me, "Can you fix it so I can fight?"

"If necessary I can numb the whole rib, but I wouldn't recommend it."

This brings about a question I have often been asked by my colleagues. How far should one stretch medical common sense and prudence in getting a fighter ready? Take this case. Ali had been granted a license. Although it had so far withstood the strongest political pressure, the fight hung on by the slimmest thread. One postponement and it could collapse on us. My responsibility was to Ali and Herbert. I felt I could block the intercostal nerve and give Ali sufficient relief from pain so he could fight Quarry for at least one hour. If I had then had the information I now have on Ali, I would not have even contemplated a nerve block, for Ali is amazingly tough. The man can stand an inordinate amount of pain in the ring, and do it stoically so that no one is aware that he is suffering. Nonetheless, at the time we were all fired up by a sort of missionary zeal. We were all working for Ali to return to the ring. Let's face it, I would have numbed *my* rib if I felt it would have helped Ali answer the bell and launch his reconquest of his stolen title.

As it turned out, the one in need of medical treatment that wonderful night in Atlanta was Jerry Quarry, who had a large laceration of the brow that I sutured after the fight. Jerry was disappointed, but he was about to embark on a remarkable career. He is the only boxer to make a successful career out of failure.

The more he lost, the more he was paid for the next fight. I like Jerry and his crazy fighting family, but I am very glad he retired when he did. Only Chuvalo could take more punishment, but then again Chuvalo had a braver manager, Irving Ungerman.

About this time Ali began to have serious problems with his hands. Out of action for three years, Ali's hands were sensitive to the pounding that he subjected them to as he began intensive training again. Hitting the heavy bag after a three-year absence made them very sore, and soon he developed a bursitis of the knuckle and at times a tendonitis. He had, in other words, sore hands. There is no solution to this problem but rest, but Ali could not rest his hands. The other solution was obvious: numb his hands and let him punch to his heart's delight.

The Oscar Bonavena fight, on a cold December night, was his next big test in the Garden. For the first time I took my syringes into the dressing room and used them *before* a fight. Taking a dentist's capsule of novocaine, I deadened Ali's knuckles so that he could punch with impunity. He made it through the fight and knocked out Oscar in the fifteenth round of an extremely hard fight. His hands held up but they were very sore thereafter. Now began a series of fights that made me an indispensable factor around the camp, and also caused me a great deal of difficulty with various factions in the camp, including Ali himself.

The most important fight of his career loomed up in the form of *The Fight:* Ali versus *Joe Frazier* for the heavy-weight title of the *World.* Ali continued to have tender hands and still could not give them the rest they needed. Again the plan was to deaden the hands. Ali did not particularly like this arrangement, but he understood that if he was to punch with any effect against the hard-charging Joe Frazier, he would not be able to worry about his hands. Herbert also was not happy with the arrangement, but he yielded to the in-evitable logic of the situation. We could not postpone the fight. Joe would come at Ali like an armored tank. Ali would need his two hands to punch, without being handi-capped by pain.

The fight proved to be every bit as good as expected. Seldom has realization exceeded expectation. As you have read in another part of this book, Ali lasted the fifteen, and the outcome is still a matter of late-night debates by people who view the film today. Following the fight, Ali was limp. To dress him required two grown men. He was absolutely exhausted. He could only rouse himself from his stupor to ask plaintively, "Was it a good fight?" Not, mind you, "Who won the fight?" but "Was it a *good* fight?"

A few of us drove in the limo to the Flower and Fifth Avenue Hospital in silence, Angelo somberly looking out of the frosted-over window. Dr. Gordon, the Miami plastic surgeon, came along to study the X-ray films for the possi-bility of a skull fracture or jaw fracture. The mood was grim. Only Ali remained in good, if exhausted, spirits. It was my first view of Ali in defeat. Was it different from what I had expected? *Yes.*

I frankly did not attribute to Ali this strength of character that is so rarely found in any man. Ali had made his mark with his frank narcissism and his big mouth. How would he react when he finally got out on a limb and it collapsed? Well, friends, he did better than most men, and certainly better than I would. He accepted it totally. He had fought and he had lost. No excuse. No alibi. No copout. "Was it a good fight?" The artist in Ali had to be satisfied. Did the people get their money's worth? That was all he wanted to know. Not, is my jaw broken? Not, I was robbed. Not, I'll get him next time. He just asked a quiet question to satisfy his artist's soul.

In spite of the most stringent security measures, we were greeted at the hospital by a small crowd of disaster watchers. I am amazed by the speed of the news media in America. Few people knew our destination, yet there at the door is George Plimpton, a concerned look on his handsome face.

Celebrities are in danger in any hospital in the world. The late night help fall all over themselves for a view, and I am distressed to say that even the young doctors are star struck. In this case we X-rayed the skull, read the films, satisfied ourselves of the absence of a fracture or hematoma, and left. So did the films. Some ghoul stole the Ali X-rays and kept them for a souvenir. And Ali refused to stay in the hospital for precautionary observation. His eye was solely on the future and posterity, mine on the malpractice courts. He won.

Following the Frazier loss Ali began his world travels, and most of the time the hands got an injection, but he was on the whole getting back to his remarkable superhuman form. Slowly his body was returning to his former condition, and amazingly enough the years seemed to be going backward. Continuous fighting got him into great shape, but his hands got worse. Only rest would help them, and finally we got help from an unexpected source. It was what one would regard as the Bad Solution to a problem—Ali fractured his jaw.

Ali, bored by continuous easy fights, took Norton cheaply. He played and he neglected to train. He talked through the first round and somewhere in the second round he took a punch with his mouth open and fractured his jaw. He returned to his corner and, as described earlier, I could move his jaw. Ali could move his jaw with his tongue! Here I pause to say that sometimes, in the desire to help one's friends, one steps in *shit*. Ali, apprised of the fact that he had a broken jaw, refused to let Angelo stop the fight. I had the power to stop it by motioning to the boxing commission doctor, but Ali was not in danger of losing his life, and the jaw was in place and not causing hemorrhaging. So, believing, as Ali and Angelo did, that he could put away Norton easily, we let it go on. After a few strange rounds I decided to help an old friend, Howard Cosell, who was doing the ringside commentary.

Many people dislike Howard Cosell because of his abrasive style on camera. Some hate him because he is his own press agent and greatest booster. Some hate him because of his fluid verbiage. Some hate him as a smart ass, overeducated New York lawyer looking down his nose at the sports figures he makes his handsome living from, whom he ridicules at the slightest chance. However, I like him. I see him in a different light and help him whenever I can because, at his best, he is a breath of fresh air in the stereotyped world of sports reporting, and basically he is a very nice man. This is not a blanket recommendation of Howard and his methods but a prelude to the following step-in-the-muck story.

As the round finished, I felt I should give Howard a chance to shine. If I indicated that something was wrong with Ali's jaw, Howard could have a field day spotting the defect and would be able to "tell it like it is" to the American public. Unfortunately, Howard did not get the simple message I communicated, and felt compelled to put a mike in front of us in the midst of the fight. Angelo regarded the mike as he would a cobra that had just been put on the top ring step.

Howard, leaning forward, shouted, "Ferdie, what is wrong with Ali's jaw? Is it broken?"

"No, it is just a chipped tooth," I answered facetiously.

Howard wouldn't take the hint. Digging, he put the mike to Angelo. "Is it busted, Angie?"

"Naw, chipped tooth," Angelo said in his absent manner. Next to Howard is Joe Frazier doing the color, and he is a good friend of Norton's. And he hates Ali. One word from Joe to the ring doctor and it is over, with Ali losing on a TKO.

Again, the stoic acceptance of pain and the inevitable is Ali's way of handling this freak piece of luck. Norton won't quit and his style is very hard for Ali to solve. As the rounds pass, Norton gets braver and braver. The crowd cannot follow what is happening. Cosell thinks he knows but cannot get anyone to confirm what is happening. Cosell's obligation is to his public and the American Broadcasting Company. Ours is solely to Muhammad Ali. We allow him to keep fighting, my conscience killing me every punch of the way, and finally it is all over and, to no one's surprise, we lose a close decision. No argument is possible. There are no points given in boxing for fighting with a broken jaw. For taking painful shots. For bravery. Ali definitely lost, and now we have the problem of fixing the jaw in San Diego.

The dressing room was sheer hysteria. In the midst of the boxing action Ali's loyal wife Belinda had suffered a hysterical attack, and then lapsed into a coma from which she did not recover for two days. The commission doctor, Lundeen of San Diego, arranged for the hospital and called in a plastic surgeon, Dr. Lancaster, who had fortunately done a lot of work with fractured jaws in Vietnam. He was a perfect choice. Both men behaved admirably and proved cool professionals. The surgery was swiftly done, only the three of us and the scrub nurse being present. In the hallway stood the ever present Angelo Dundee and Gene Kilroy. The manager, Herbert, was back at the stadium, doing his best to take care of Belinda. He was in touch continuously, although the rest of the camp followers dissolved into the night.

The next day a red-eyed Herbert, Angelo, and I returned to the hospital. Ali was alone except for a bodyguard in the hall, stationed there chiefly to keep a crazy lady and her daughter from coming in to bother Ali. Ali was just out of the recovery room and he was feeling the pain of the surgery. His jaw was wired together, and his face was drawn from the nonstop pain he was suffering. Gingerly we approached, each with a speech in his mind to relieve Ali of his hurt feelings, to console him about the defeat, to reassure him about continuing in the fight business until he got his title back. Ali regarded us with his famous twinkling eyes and waved us to sit down. He said, "Now what are you looking so down about? It is just a little broken bone. I put men in the hospital before. Now it is my turn to go to the hospital. That is the way it is in boxing, man, don't be down. I will come back, and I want Norton first. Get me that chump before he gets knocked off by somebody. Herbert, it is just another test Allah puts before us. Accept it as that. It is Allah's will—now we will overcome this—you wait and see. Angie, other boxers fought after they broke their jaws, so will I. Don't worry. You did a good job, Doc. Don't worry, I will rest, the hands will be better and I will get that rest you are always bugging me about."

I have to regard Ali in a new light. Again he has fooled me. How long is it going to take me to realize that this is an *unusual* human being. Here we are trying to comfort him and *he* is comforting *us*. Incredible. Not a whimper, not

a question, not a request for a pain killer. No, he is concerned
wtih *our* suffering. I am not only speechless but afraid that if
I speak I will cry, which is both embarrassing and very
unprofessional.

Finally our pain is over with in San Diego. Belinda recovers and returns to her old steady reliable self, full of good
humor and joyous vibes and happy to have her man to herself
for six months. Ali is in good hands. He has a happy home,
and doing six months in that home is doing good time. I fix
him up with a Philadelphia plastic surgeon and return to my
own practice and life. But complications unthought of await
me before we can get Ali back in the ring with Norton.

Ali has a molar missing at the point of fracture. Indeed,
the missing molar contributed to the weakness at that point
in his jaw, and that weakness, plus a freak pressure applied
from a lucky punch, broke the jaw. As soon as it has set well,
I have Ali come down to Miami and go to a pair of dentists
who understand this type of work, because they are the
dentists for the Dolphins football team. The Teshers, Bob
and Fred, are superior professionals and I know we are in
good hands. Ali is a very good patient and the Teshers are
thrilled to have him as a patient. The bridge is made and the
jaw looks much stronger than ever before. Everything looks
serene, but I did not count on the Iagos of this strange camp.

C. B. Atkins had worked out a deal with some Asian
potentates to have Ali fight in Dakarta, Indonesia, in the
Fall, and accepted a little taste up front. There was a com-
plication, however, and it was a big one. What if Ali fought
in September in L.A. against Norton and his jaw broke again?
The Indonesia fight would be out, and C. B. would have to
return the money. I am sure that the thought of passing over
Norton to go straight to Dakarta occurred to some of these
people involved in this deal; however, Ali was set on fighting
Norton and avenging the loss. Intrigue took over.

C. B. Atkins and Richard Durham, Ali's ghost writer, were genuinely concerned that Ali's jaw would not hold up, and they were also concerned about his hands. Well-meaning people had taken Ali to a country doctor in the hills of Pennsylvania next to his camp. He had dragged out the old country remedy of soaking Ali's hands in warm paraffin (wax) to relieve the soreness. The fact was that his hands were already better because of the rest he had given them. Nonetheless, taking advantage of this hook, C. B. convinced Herbert to let him take Ali to a Boston hospital to consult a hand surgeon there. The orthopedist agreed with my diagnosis and prognosis, and there was nothing to be done there. However, C. B. figured, once there, why not have his jaw looked at by a plastic surgeon. Fate took a hand now. The surgeon was out, so why not go to the dental clinic? The head of the dental clinic was out, so why not go to the dental residents? Two eager young dentists proceeded to agree with C. B.: Bottom line, Ali could not fight much before *December,* and this was in early July!

At this point I was called on the red alert phone by Bob Arum who had set up the L.A. Norton fight for September. Mad as hell, I wondered why anyone who wanted to was allowed to take Ali anywhere to get examined by anyone. My temper out of the way, I got to thinking. Who was the top expert on jaw fractures in the world? I called several plastic surgeons and got the same answers. The top expert was Reed Dingman, M.D., of the University of Michigan. I called and got an appointment for Ali to see him after a great deal of argument with his dragon-lady nurse. I had to go to Europe for another fight, and I left it to Ali's people to get him there.

Upon my return I learned to my dismay that Ali had not gone to see the good doctor. Nor had he called to break the appointment, which was the greater of the sins in the eyes of the nurse, who had her own viewpoint of who was the celebrity in that matchup. Again Arum called, very upset. This time, I said, let's all go to see the good doctor en masse. But getting the appointment was even harder than the first time. The nurse was downright hostile, and I must say I did not blame her. I explained to her that I had been in Europe at the time of the appointment, and that I would certainly have called her to cancel. No one else did, but there were unusual circumstances. The week of the appointment was the week that Major Coxson—who had been getting very chummy with Ali as his financial advisor—and his family went west, or bought the farm, as they say. There were rumors that the major was dealing in drugs and, what with one thing or the other, time ran out on him and he met his end. Ali was moved from Cherry Hill, near the massacre site, to Chicago, where his people could watch him closely and keep him away from what could be dangerous territory. In the ensuing hoo-haa, the last thing on anybody's mind was an appointment in Michigan.

Fortunately the nurse bought that version, and we made our appointment for Thursday, my normal day off. I flew to New York on Wednesday night and stayed with Bob Arum at his home in Scarsdale. The next morning we flew to Detroit to meet Ali and Herbert, and get the final decision from the great jaw mensch in Michigan. Viewing the highly irregular behavior of C. B. in all this, I wanted Herbert to hear the verdict with his own ears. Imagine my surprise when I got off at Detroit to be met by Ali, his daughter, and C. B. Atkins, but no Herbert Muhammad. Bob Arum shook his head and we moved toward the rental car to make the drive to the campus.

The drive was marked by a bullshit barrage from C. B. aimed at Ali, telling him how much we all thought of him and his jaw, and how all any of us wanted was for his jaw to be right. In view of the fact that two out of three of us stood to profit greatly out of Ali's fighting, I pointed out that just possibly I was the only one there with an altruistic motive. C. B. squirmed uncomfortably and protested to Ali, "I don't get nothing out of this, Ali, I just want to see you get well and not risk breaking your jaw again by fighting too soon."

Both Arum and I let out a laugh. My god, C. B. had not hit a lick of work since he latched on to the Ali Circus ten years back. I couldn't resist. *"You don't get anything out of this, C. B.?* What have you been living off, the air?"

At this, Ali let out a yelp and hit C. B. on the shoulder. "You hear that, you ghetto nigger, you hear the Doc? You been living off the air, C. B.? That's a good one, Doc, living off the air. What do you know 'bout jaws, C. B.? How you going to argue with the Doc? You are a dumb ghetto nigger and he is smart and educated. You shut up, C. B." Ali hit C. B. again and went off into a mirthful chuckle. Ali loves to cause divisiveness, and I knew C. B. would dislike me thereafter.

We arrived at the campus of the great university a full half hour ahead of time. We parked in front of the doctor's office. The place looked like a Norman Rockwell painting of a small town: neat, small clapboard house typical of the Midwest in the mid-forties. Across the street was a fairly large hospital.

All of us were on edge and in a bad mood when Ali said brightly, "Let's get some coffee in that hospital."

I jumped out of my skin. "Are you crazy, Ali, we are supposed to be here in greatest secrecy. I don't want anyone to know you were here today, or what you are here for."

Lightly jumping over my objections and the front seat, Ali strode across the small street and into the hospital. Instant pandemonium in the cafeteria. Yelps of delight from the black help, and bashful stares from the white employees.

Fifteen minutes are passed in good-natured bantering and autograph signing until, at last, on the edge of the crowd, a little white lady speaks to Ali, who has to bend his huge frame to hear her. Tearfully, she asks if Ali will come up to the neurology ward to see her son and cheer up some of the inmates. Ali jumps up and the three of us go up to the neurology ward.

The neurology ward of any hospital is a grabber. Most of the patients are in some form of paralysis. This young 18-year-old patient was paralyzed from his neck down. A few months before he had rolled his sports car over and snapped a cervical vertebra. There was no hope for a recovery.

The young kid lit up like a Christmas tree when he saw Ali. Ali approached in a shocked condition, but covered up by joking and jiving with the kid. They spoke for a long time. The kid asked him to see the other inmates and Ali turned around to tell him to keep punching and fighting, that things would be all right, but when he tried to go on his voice caught and he could not finish. Recovering quickly, he spotted a black janitor with a broom and started sparring and carrying on with him, which brightened up everyone's day. And then we left, as suddenly and unexpectedly as we came, leaving a stunned but temporarily cheered bunch of unfortunates.

In the elevator Ali turned to me. "You mean he ain't *never* going to walk, or get over that? *Not ever?*"

"No, he is not. He is there forever."

"Now, *that* is sumptin. Now that is sumptin to think about, not this nothing jaw of mine. Let's go see what the Doc says."

So we walked to the doctor's office, where I turned to Bob Arum and said, "I don't want anyone in with us but Ali and the doctor. Walk C. B. around the block."

Dr. Dingman is a rather tall, straight-laced looking man, pleasant, courteous, and, with his button-down shirt collar and thin tie, looking like a movie-type casting of a 1948 general practitioner. He was straightforward and very impressive. He began by a quick review of the X-rays and history of the fracture. He knew the surgeon who operated on Ali and endorsed him fully. Now we were ready for the exam. I stopped him and said, "Doctor, immediately following his examination, in front of Ali, you tell him your opinion. Yes or no, can he fight in September or not. Give it to him straight. I will not tell you what I think."

Ali sat passively listening to all this, and then got examined by the doctor so vigorously I thought he was going to refracture the jaw.

"Hell, this man can fight *this* month if he wants to." And, so saying, he gave the jaw a nice smart whack with his closed fist. I envisioned a reflexive counter by Ali to the liver. At that moment I looked out of the window to see a sweating C. B. and a miserable looking Arum walking around the block for their hundredth turn.

Once outside we were all ecstatic. Well, three out of the four of us were ecstatic. C. B. was smiling bravely, trying to act as if that was good news, but his jolly face seemed ready to melt into tears.

Now began the insidious Battle of the Camp. C. B. and Durham were still not convinced. Kilroy had doubts. They wanted Ali to go here, to go there, to see this guy and that, but Ali held firm and we went with Dr. Dingman's and my opinion. I had the feeling that my own health was in jeopardy if Ali's jaw did, in fact, fracture.

An interesting note to demonstrate the divisiveness of the camp occurred at this time. Late one night, Hal Conrad and Budd Schulberg were getting into an elevator and were joined by Gene Kilroy. Gene was genuinely concerned about the jaw and said so to Budd, but he also said he thought that the bridge I had the dentists put in was a bad idea, and that the jaw would break sooner. There was that unspoken implication that I might either not know what I was doing or even might be, in effect, doing something slightly irregular. This prompted an outburst from Budd, and Kilroy backed down. The next day Budd was still steamed, but I told him that this was the way that things had become in the Ali Circus.

The second Norton fight was very hard, Ali winning by a superior effort in the last round. The jaw did not break and has not caused difficulties since then. The hands were getting better and better, and we were getting to another crossroads which would mark the change in my relation to Ali.

Details were worked out and we started moving to the second Frazier fight. The first fight had been a classic, but since then Ali had slipped, and Frazier had given his rendition of a bouncing basketball with Frazier as the bouncing ball and Foreman as the ballplayer. The bloom was off the rose, but Joe Frazier was still Joe Frazier.

Herbert now began to question me about the effect of these hand shots. I explained that they only numbed the knuckles so that Ali could punch hard through the fight, but had nothing to do with the speed or accuracy of the punch, and had no lasting effect on Ali. Herbert seemed convinced, but a few days later was again skeptical. I told him that the sooner Ali could do without the shots the better I would feel since, as I have always said, the less you do for a fighter the better. However, on this particular occasion, Frazier made things a different matter. To fight Frazier you required strong hands, and while Ali's hands were getting better, they were not *that* well. Herbert nodded inconclusively.

It is well to mention something about Herbert Muhammad here. He is seldom written about because he maintains a low profile and does not care for or seek publicity. Herbert started out with Ali new to the fight game. In no time he picked up all the details, and eventually came on to dispel the picture of a phony "up front" kind of a man. Herbert does what he says he is going to do. His handshake is better than a million signed contracts. He is honest with his employees and tries to do the best for everyone after he first takes care of Ali, which is exactly as it should be. He has been elected Manager of the Year, and they could just have easily made that the Decade. Herbert is not so perfect that he cannot be influenced by members of the camp, but generally he listens to all, observes quietly, and draws his own conclusions from the actions and not the words of people. I had not had one problem with Herbert, and the question of the shade of my skin had never come up. Now it did, with a queer result.

When the time came for me to work on Ali's hands, Ali called me into the cubicle we were to use. "Doc, you know I trust you, but . . . the Boys in Chicago . . ." His voice trailed off.

"Ali, you need this to fight Frazier. What are you saying?"

"Well, the Boys from Chicago say no one knows what you are putting into my hands. You're white and you don't get paid, so they may be able to buy you off and then you put some dope in my hands. . . . *I trust you, Doc,* but *they* say how can you trust a white man that don't get paid." He looked at his white shoes bleakly.

"The hell with it then. Don't put anything in your hands. It's your ass that Frazier is going to eat up, not mine. Get them to numb your hands."

"No, you can do it, Doc, but they want you to use *their* stuff." And with this he produced a small unlabeled vial of unknown material.

"Hell no, pal, I either put what I know is good and fresh in you or nothing. I am not about to put anything in your hands that I am not sure of, especially from people I don't know. Forget it totally or do it yourself."

Ali saw I was steaming, and he took a second to shrug it off. "Doc, you do it your way."

The fight was tough and hard and Ali won going away,

punching with impunity. To his credit he sought me out as the decision was announced and panted in my ear, "I couldn't have done it without you, Doc."

At home after that episode I reflected on the bizarre qualities of human nature. The fact that I worked for nothing in boxing marked me as suspect. It didn't matter that I had an unblemished record in boxing medicine, that I had more experience than any ring doctor in history, that I worked with seven different champions, not just Ali, and had never charged a fee from any of them. That did not seem to count. The fact that I had never been wrong in my medical judgments with Ali, had backed him to the hilt in his exile years, and struggled to get him back the title did not count. What did count was that I was white and working free, therefore automatically suspect. I do not think that the people who count, in this case Herbert and Ali, felt this way, but nonetheless there it was. In order to be trustworthy I must charge a fee. The bigger the fee, presumably, the more trustworthy I would be, and parenthetically, the better a doctor I would be. After a brief struggle with my conscience I submitted a mammoth bill.

My bell rang in a few days' time and it was Bob Arum who was then handling the paymaster chores. He was laughing easily and said, "Guess what? I am convinced that you can't figure boxing people out. Herbert saw your bill and said that *it wasn't enough!* He is authorizing me to add some more on."

Since that fight I have been paid for my ministrations to Ali, although I have never again submitted a bill since I leave it to Herbert to decide what is right. Let's face it, I would be glad to *pay him* for the honor of working with the greatest fighter that ever lived. I am at heart a dyed-in-the-wool boxing fan, and up to then I have never accepted a cent from any fighter or his managers in return for my corner work and medical attentions. I had not only treated fighters without a fee, but their families as well, and was happy to do so. Ali caused me to break my streak, but if doing so made them trust me more, then so be it.

Now that I was a hired hand in the Ali Circus, I prepared to go to Africa for the final step in the reconquest of the title. You have read how that turned out in another part of this book, but I must go into the strange efforts of a fellow doctor to enter into the picture, and what potentially dangerous efforts it almost had on the most important fight of Ali's comeback career.

Herbert had called me to go to Zaire and, as an aside, had told me he was inviting his family doctor, who had been treating his ailing father, Elijah Muhammad. He specified that this would in no way interfere with my duties and authority over the boxing part of Ali's life. I knew that this could not stay this simple since, as I said before, people are drawn to Ali for various reasons, mostly for selfish reasons, but also because he makes one feel that one is helping him. The heady combination of the first world title fight between two black men, promoted by a black man, in the middle of the mother country, Africa, got to the black Chicago medic faster than it takes to tell it. I never show up for a fight until, at the most, five to six days beforehand. The good doctor beat me there by several weeks, and this was enough to allow him to take over the medical duties of the camp. By the time I appeared on the scene, he had convinced the camp that Ali suffered from low blood sugar—technically hypoglycemia.

Frankly, hypoglycemia is a catchall diagnosis like hypertension, used to justify various reasons for weakness. Ali was getting dizzy following workouts, and he felt tired. The fact that he was in a tropical climate, training hard at midday, and well past thirty did not occur to anyone, except for the experienced boxing people like Dundee and Sarria. But, as usual, they were powerless to stop those camp members who are so good at ingratiating themselves by pointing out nonexistent bugaboos. Ali, left alone, will adjust and slowly forget his complaints and when the bell rings the Ali batteries will be fully charged. I repeat for the hundredth time, the less you do to a fighter the better. Overtreatment also serves to psych the fighter into thinking he is carrying a burden into the ring. In much the same way that Angelo never permits the word "tired" to be said in the corner, I feel the word "sick" should be banned from the camp. As long as a good doctor who knows fighters is watching the progress of the fighter, and has his finger on the pulse of the training camp program, you do not have much to worry about. In Ali's case all hangers-on are trying to justify their position in camp, or jockey for a better position, so they are overly concerned and are always bringing in certain types to "find out what is wrong with the champ" and offer their bizarre cures. To Ali's credit, he listens but infrequently does what is suggested. Ali is a survivor.

The diagnosis of low blood sugar was not substantiated by any lab work, and it is basically a laboratory diagnosis. The cure, if the disease is indeed proven, is a dietary one. The apparent cure to the layman would be to put more gas in the tank. If the tank needs sugar, add more sugar; however, *that is the last thing one should do!* Indeed, it provokes the body to overreact, causing much greater sugar deficiency. Keep that point in mind clearly, for we are about to see how little things can affect big happenings.

Upon my arrival in Zaire, I was introduced to the Chicago doctor, who proved to be a very pleasant man, with a sort of apologetic, preoccupied air. He told me what he had found and what he proposed doing about it. The solution was this: The night of the fight he had ordered the cook to bake a large apple cobbler and pour honey all over the top. This deep dish delicacy he would feed Ali one hour before ring time. The prevailing thought was that *that* would *surely put gas in the tank!*

I looked at him in amazement. Now I have not lasted in the Ali Circus this long because I am indiscreet and straightforward with these people. So courteously I explained that while this might be feasible in his Chicago clinic, it would not work in Africa because we are dealing with a fighter about to get his midsection pummeled by a leveling force comparable to the H-bomb—namely, George Foreman, known for his devastating body attack. To feed this gooey mess to Ali one hour before the fight would be dangerous. He agreed, but hesitantly proposed a sugar-saturated orange juice substitute, which I reluctantly accepted as an alternative, feeling like Chamberlain must have felt at Munich.

The dilemma was maddening because I had to respect the likable little doctor, who was trying his best. The respect was due him because he was Herbert Muhammad's doctor, and was taking care of the Honorable Elijah Muhammad, Herbert's father, and Ali's spiritual leader. I was not about to demean him, or to accuse him of incompetence. The fact that he was a black doctor also entered into it, because I did not want to be accused of racial bias, and of lowering the professional status of a black man. I felt that in due time he would overextend himself and go the way of so many who have been in the Ali Circus, but meantime we had George Foreman to think of, and I would not allow anything to jeopardize Ali's chances.

Ali's hand had gotten much better, so there was also a lot of discussion about whether to inject it again. Ali, as always, was considerate of me, thinking he would hurt my feelings if it were not done. He had it in his mind that numbing a knuckle affected his speed and accuracy, a thought gradually placed there by the camp masterminds. While I do not believe that this is medically possible, I do feel that if Ali was thinking this way then it *was* affecting him adversely. I told him so, and further told him I thought the whole thing overblown since his hands were in good shape except for the main knuckle on his right hand. That one knuckle we could do alone if necessary; meanwhile, many conferences were held, all without conclusions being drawn. In the end it was between Ali and me alone, and he chose to forget it this time and ride out the pain with his abundant courage and his super charge of natural adrenalin. I agreed, and also talked him out of even thinking about the pie before the fight, which idea had been broached to him. He seemed wistful as he gave it up, because if there is a great temptation in Ali's life it is sweets. He adores pie and ice cream. However, the thought of the pounding he was going to take in the mid-digestion area was enough to convince him to forget that move. The little doctor was nothing if not persistent, and we had that idea come up again before each of the next two fights.

Finally, the compromise sugar-saturated bottle of orange juice was accepted, and we put the bottle in the corner bucket, with the normal water bottle. Since Angelo handles the water, and we two privately agreed to pass up the orange juice idea, we got through the fight without having to put that dangerous idea to a test. Ali won the title that night, and I have to say that it was one of the highest moments of my life. To have been a part of that long uphill reconquest was a thrill I do not expect to duplicate in sports if I stay in it for thirty more years.

Back in the States I waited until Ali came to Miami to train. I called Belinda, and also Herbert, and told them that since Ali would not go to the doctor in Chicago, the doctor would come to him. I told Ali not to eat anything at all in the morning and come to the gym to train. Now it was boiling hot in Miami, and Ali worked a good two-hour stint. As the doctor got through examining him, I trapped him in the cubicle, drew a large sample of blood, and took a urine sample. These I rushed over to the lab and did a complete

analysis. Just as I suspected: *No hypoglycemia.* Jubilantly
I phoned Herbert and Belinda, and they were very happy.
Finally, I thought, we're rid of that red herring. We were
preparing to go to Malaysia and Joe Bugner, and I felt the
matter was closed. Wrong.

Upon my arrival in Kuala Lumpur, the first face I see is
that of our colleague from Chicago, with his wife. Again,
Herbert says they are just invited guests. Again, I remind
Herbert to keep him out of the boxing end of this camp, but I
hear the same stories about low blood sugar, and about
home remedies to cure this. Again, the compromise with the
orange juice comes up and it is beginning to be painfully
funny. Now I am not laughing, but anyhow Joe Bugner is not
George Foreman, and we have a little leeway for error. The
good doctor has caught the flavor and fever of being an Ali
Circus follower, and he has brought his wife two weeks ahead
of time. The fight ends up favorably for us and I dismiss the
episode entirely.

Manila and Joe Frazier come next, this time the good
doctor comes with Ali as part of the entourage; he is much
more active, emboldened by the experience of surviving two
expeditions with the craziest of the Ali camp. Now he is
treating all of the camp. Herbert maintains his position that
he can do what he wants as an invited guest, but should not
interfere with Ali. The morning of the fight I come into the
dressing room to see a pastry box full of napoleons, cream
confectioneries, and an assortment of Danish. The hypoglycemia ploy still hasn't died. I solve this problem by passing
the pastry out to the crews and our camp followers. Thank
heavens Ali abstains, because he has the fight of his life
awaiting him with the magnificent machine that is Joe
Frazier, who is *not* suffering from hypoglycemia.

The sweet end to this story comes the day after the fight.
The invited guest sees fit to hand Herbert a small reminder

of his friendship and appreciation of favors past. This reminder is in the form of a substantial bill. Now it is Herbert's turn to feel weak and dizzy. Suffice it to say that Herbert, not being known as a spendthrift and fool, cut the bill down to size. And so it goes in the Ali Circus.

14·The Real Ali

The most frequent question I am asked by people regarding Ali is, "What is Ali *really* like?" It is an unanswered question for the simple reason that Ali almost defies description. Ali gives many people the feeling that they know him intimately, only to show them a totally unexpected side of himself and fool them again and again. The only predictable thing about Ali is his unpredictability, which is a characteristic in itself.

Ali, it is universally conceded among the Ali watchers, is a mass of contradictions, forever changing according to the circumstances and the pressures. He is most basically a *reactor*. He reacts to most things at a gut level. He does not spend a great deal of time in making agonizing intellectual decisions. Ali fires from the hip, and leaves a wake of startled people once again readjusting their thinking on him. Most of his decisions are made on the spur of the moment, depending on who is bending his ear at the time. If the person trying to influence him is not to his immediate liking he may decide simply to irritate that person, and on the other hand he may decide in favor of following the advice of a friend he likes, or doesn't want to hurt, even though it is not in his best interests at the time.

Although I do not believe Ali capable of any great prolonged intellectual thought process, I do feel he has a quality, that is so mysterious and inaccessible to 90 percent of the human race, of doing the right thing by gut feeling alone. He has the quality of obstinacy, and this infuriates the smart guys. If he thinks he is right he will stick to his guns, and, by all that's holy, in the end he is usually proven correct. The most infuriating thing is that he intuitively does the right thing, but for the wrong reason. Here's an early example of what I mean.

When Cassius Clay first triumphed in the Olympics, the wise guys smirked, shifted their cigars, and said, "Wait till this loud mouth hits the pros; what a beating he is going to take." Cassius came up to the Fifth Street Gym and the comments were the same. What was he doing wrong? He held his hands low, by his hips, he pulled back from a punch so far that he appeared out of balance, he punched while on his tiptoes, he ignored his opponent's body like it was off limits. Obviously he had disobeyed all the tenets that go to make up a good fighter. The savants were theoretically right, but they discounted the remarkable faculties of Cassius Clay. His body was long and lithe, he had the hands and foot speed of a fast welterweight, he had the boxing brain of a Willie Pep, an instinct, that I am convinced is born in a fighter, to know where the punches are coming from and how to avoid them. He possessed such an awesomely accurate punch that he did not need to soften up an opponent's body so that his guard would drop and punches to the head would land. He did not need body punches, his shots landed cleanly on the head of the opponent without exposing himself to counterpunches. A hard body attack leaves the attacker open to be counterpunched silly. Witness Marciano, Frazier, and numerous others.

Ali's six-foot-three-inch frame and his reflexive speed made it impossible to hit him when he leaned back. His feet carried him out of harm's way, and his blinding hand speed made the opponent pay an awesome price to chase him to the ropes. And if he ever did corral Ali in a corner or on the ropes, Ali utilized all these qualities to escape harm and then turn about and punch his adversary silly. Clearly, here was a fighting machine that could not be improved. Ali instinctively was a great fighter at the very time he turned pro. One could refine but not alter his style. Not that everyone didn't try, because it takes a very smart man to recognize genius in the raw, but Ali, in the first of his right gut moves, would nod and then proceed to do what he wanted without regard for the advice. It is also fortunate that Ali had a great boxing man to complement him in his ambitions, and that man was Angelo Dundee. Angelo quit trying to change what was working so well, and confined himself to polishing his fighter's style and picking the right quality opponents. One of a manager's chief functions is to pick opponents intelligently for his young fighter. They must be stepping stones. The fighter must learn something with every fight, polish, and improve, but he must not be overmatched against a cagey veteran, or a much better fighter, or in a hopeless hometown situation early in the game. Cassius Clay was beautifully managed in his early years. Later, when he became Muhammad Ali, it would not make any difference, for he was head and shoulders above the rest of the field. They would have to go to Mars to find an opponent to fear.

His second major right-but-apparently-wrong move was his position on the draft. Did Ali arrive at this on his own, or was this a Muslim edict that he had to follow? No one but Ali and Herbert will ever know, but I feel that it is safe to assume it was at the very least a joint decision. Not even Elijah Muhammad, the man most influential in Ali's life, could *fully* control Ali. Ali was distrustful of the white man's world and authority, and certainly he would have been under the gun in the army. He was a symbol of *black is best* in the world. He did not want anything to do with whites or their world, and suddenly he would have been in what is almost a pure white man's world, under absolute orders, to serve as totally as his forefathers served their masters. No, Muhammad Ali did not want any part of that world. All the smart advisors told him to go. What would he lose? He would spend the two years doing boxing exhibitions, and the army would have allowed a title fight every six months. Probably so, but Ali did not want to take that chance, and he felt like he would rather accept the consequences. A lot of claptrap has been written about his political foresight, his political beliefs, his protest against the Vietnam war, his brave disregard of certain imprisonment. Baloney. Ali is an apolitical animal. He is an instinctual animal. He just didn't want to go. Damn the consequences. He just didn't want to go. As it turned out, it was perhaps the turning point in his life. He went from famous fighter to famous *international figure*. Ali could not guess that this move would turn out so well. All of us who went out trying to get Ali a license, who tried to help during the exile years, met with the raw hatred and resentfulness of middle America. We were rebuffed in almost every state in the Union, but every time I went to Europe I saw the admiration and respect that was building up for Ali. And gradually in this country, in the streets of the ghetto, and in the universities, people were responding to his stance. What had appeared a Don Quixote move at first began to appear like the Crusades.

The third move occurred sometime after the first Frazier fight, and might have been as a consequence of it. As you have read, the first fight was a nightmare of crowd hysteria. No place to train, no place to hide from the ever demanding public. Ali was doing more show biz schtick than training. It might have cost him that fight. Immediately after, it became apparent that Miami Beach was not the place for Ali. He was too big. The crowds had become out of control. He needed privacy. Fortunately, Ali had at his side an unusual member of the Ali Circus. In another dizzying turn of his character, Ali had picked as his close friend and confidant, a white man in the form of the personable Gene Kilroy. No one knows why, since Ali trusts and likes blacks, and is skeptical of white men. You read about his distrust of Angelo in the first Liston fight, and of my ministrations in the second Frazier fight. He got rid of Bob Arum, although he is gifted and highly talented, and was good for Ali. Only Kilroy rode serene over the waves of camp criticism and even dislike. Somehow he had Ali's ear, which is yet another example of Ali's remarkable perversity. To get back to the point, Gene came up with a great real estate deal in the woods of Pennsylvania, near a hamlet called Deerlake. Ali would have to come up with a sizable amount of cash, and then spend a great deal more to build a training camp on top of an inaccessible mountain. The brains scoffed: there were a million things against it. First, Ali thrived on public exposure, and this place was in the boondocks. Then it would be hard for the foxes he so adored to find him. He would have to confine himself strictly to training since there would be no outside diversions, movie houses, interviews, running around. No, Muhammad Ali, the inexhaustible playboy, would not be happy there, and pretty soon he would tire of it and lose the whole bundle. Suffice it to point out that, ever since, he stayed there, training hard for his fights, and the place is the main thing responsible for his remarkable conditioning. Ali really gets *down* in that mountain retreat, and all the things pointed out as drawbacks turned out to be advantages. He is not distracted, but if he is bored he does not show it. On the other hand, the rest of the camp acts as if they are in Devil's Island waiting for a method of escape to present itself, even though the camp itself is a truly beautiful locale for a retreat. Ali finds things to do: one day he decided to paint the huge boulders that flank the camp with the names of great past heavyweight champions. He was busily expanding on the idea of having the champs come up as his guests and each pose by his respective rock, and he was naming off the rocks: Dempsey, Louis, Marciano, Tunney, Johnson . . .

A bemused scribe looked up and said to Ali, "But Johnson is dead."

"Well, he won't have to do nothing," said Ali, not missing a beat.

The fourth move is a rather personal one, not having to do with his boxing career, so it does not enter into his professional career decisions as such, although I do think the choice of a wife is a very important career move. Cassius Clay married Sonjie in a surprise move. Sonjie was a beautiful, vivacious, semitalented girl from the streets of Chicago. They fell violently in love and never parted until they married. Then Clay became Ali and Sonjie stayed Sonjie. She did not fit the Muslim mold, and again Ali went with his gut feeling, which time and again had proven right. Ali, heartsick and truly broken up, banished Sonjie, who fought a long and costly retreating, delaying action. Ali paid through the nose for his gut feeling, in dollars and sleepless nights, but in the end he saved himself a lot of grief and heartache. No one that looks like Ali can stay single long, and his next wife proved to be what any man dreams of having for a wife.

Muhammad Ali met the beautiful teenage daughter of a high Muslim official working in a bakery shop. Her name was Belinda and she was the type of woman found in storybooks. She was a tall, statuesque young lady, with a haunting smile, laughing eyes, and a strong personality to go with the dreamboat looks. She was a Muslim through and through. She dressed to conform with the customs, was indoctrinated into what a good Muslim woman should be, wore no makeup (which, incidentally, she didn't need), and had a laughing, mischievous sense of fun that Ali likes. Ali had met his match, and he lost no time in seeing to it that it became a match. Now, years later, it seems to me that it was a magnificent move for Ali. Only a made-for-Ali woman like Belinda could have helped him through those difficult years.

But a man's personal life is his own and I do not know what the future holds for these two exceptional people. I wish them both well, together or separately.

I am purposely leaving for the last example the most important and controversial decision in Ali's life. Ali, as you've read, was converted into being a Black Muslim before the first Liston fight. There wasn't one non-Muslim person who thought that this was not the end of Ali. But consider, in hindsight, how beneficial this turned out to be for Ali at that point in his life. He was about to go down the drain into which sudden great fame and fortune so often throws a person, when these serious, dedicated people gave him the way to go: direction, guidance, discipline (of a sort), and dedication to a cause. The cause of black people. Now that the revolution is abating a bit from the fierce stands of the sixties, and the Muslims are even admitting that *not all* white people are devils, it is not so easy to see that their tough black *only* stand was best for blacks at that time. Blacks needed actively to seek an identity as blacks. Proud to be black. Better to be black. Don't want *nothing* white, gimme *black*. Ali was their showcase and their entrée into respectability. No longer were they to be considered a lunatic fringe group. An aura of respectability descended on them, and bit by bit they began to drop the *burn-the-joint-down* stance, as respectability and full coffers meant that what they were burning down was their own property. Ali brought publicity and recognition, and in return he received direction and purpose. It gave him a regime that was to keep him healthy and youthful to the present day. The Muslim move that originally appeared suicidal, ended up in probably saving Ali from the frequent ruination of the ghetto famous, and instead propelled him into the world spotlight and helped keep him there.

Ali assuredly has a knack for picking out what is good for him in the face of conflicting opinion, and I think I have made the point clear. Case rests.

Is Ali a smart man? Let us begin by saying that there are many types of smart men, and Ali is one type. As far as the educated type of smartness, Ali is less than normal. He barely reads and is hopeless about mathematical things. He cannot reason in a logical, intellectual, deductive fashion. He is not a great thinker, but an instinctual gut man. He has figured out long ago that he can hire brains, and all he has to do is his own thing to keep the coffers full. There is nothing wrong with his street sense. He is also, like many a successful man, a man that dominates his field. He knows more in that arena than any other man. What is his field? World heavyweight boxing champion? No, nothing that narrow. World celebrity! That is his field, and he will play it long after the final bell has sounded on his spectacular career. Given this constricted view, and realizing that he does not aspire to more, one has to admit that Ali is head and shoulders above all others in this class. He is a genius at publicity. A genius at saying the right thing. A genius at getting along with the public. This is the forte. I've often said that Ali could address a Ku Klux Klan rally in Mississippi and come away with an honorary sheet bestowed on him by a cheering majority. The man is a charmer. Of course it helps that he is such an imposing figure of a man, and that his accomplishments match his mouth. He is the ultimate in heroes—the Heavyweight Champion of the Whole Wide World (as he is fond of saying).

Can Ali talk? An absurd question on the surface, isn't it? Yes, but can he really talk? Converse? Exchange ideas, debate a point, enjoy a stimulating exchange of viewpoints and ideas. Can he? No.

Most conversations with Ali are monologues. Ali sends, but Ali does not receive. A man constantly deluged with newspeople requesting interviews builds a word barrier. Most questions are answered in so predictable a fashion that almost any of us in camp can do a duet with him on the answers. His catchy poems and snappy rejoinders work because they come from the great man himself, and he is as unabashed at repeating a tired doggerel to the president of an undeveloped country as George Burns is of singing vaudeville choruses on a talk show. They work for both of them for the same reason: it is a question of who says it and how. People almost ask for the gag by feeding Ali the straight line, and they delight in his answer, said for the millionth time as if it were the first. But through all the patented show biz schtick the genuine sweet nature of Ali shines through and makes it work. He truly loves, and wants to be loved in return. If he is hounded by thousands of strangers and resorts to doggerel as a defense, who can blame him? If you want to talk to Ali you must talk to him one-on-one, without an audience. To accomplish this you must put him in a car and drive him somewhere. Private talks are few and far between. Do not look for meaningful discussion for you will be disappointed. He is not a deep thinker, and sees no reason to clutter up his act with heavy thought. He sleeps well at night. He eats well. He has no need of disturbing doubts. All is straight ahead with the Ali Circus. Ali's level of thought is very primary. I am hungry, I will eat. I am cold, I will put on a coat. I want that girl, I will have her. I don't want to go to Vietnam, I won't go. I want to be a Muslim, I will be a Muslim. No room for doubt, no room for introspection. Everything is on top. He is not a deep man, although people who do not understand the phenomenon that is Ali ascribe to him qualities that he not only doesn't have but doesn't even understand.

Ali is a very secure individual, as well his accomplishments entitle him to be. My own healthy exposure to theatrical, show, and movie people, politicians, and a lot of athletes tells me that most remain basically insecure in spite of their accomplishments. Not so Ali; he is secure in his identity. He is *Numero Uno* personality in the world, and he does not doubt it for a minute. During his exile years, when pickings were slim, and the public was forgetting him day by day, Ali was riding one time in a limo in New York with an English promoter, discussing his comeback possibilities and his drawing power. Ali had about two thousand dollars in his pocket, and he asked that the limousine be stopped. He handed the wad to the Englishman and told him that he was going to walk a block down Broadway. He would not speak, would not wave, would not attract attention in any way, but would walk quietly down the street for a block. If he did not attract a crowd by the time he reached the far corner, the Englishman would not have to return the money to him. Ali descended at the corner. He began to walk. Cab drivers began to shout, truck drivers stopped their vans, shopkeepers came out to wave, and by the time he had reached the other corner he had created a traffic jam. Bear in mind that this was during his most unpopular phase, and during the time he was not seen in public for three years in a professional capacity.

Ali is a very trustworthy individual. Of course one can afford to be, given his wealth, but that is not what I refer to here. I mean he is professionally responsible. If he gives his word, you can rely on it. It takes an unusual circumstance for him to disappoint anyone when he has promised to be somewhere. A recent story serves to illustrate the point. After the Zaire fight, where Ali regained the Heavyweight Championship of the Whole Wide World, he signed to do an exhibition for Jarvis Astaire, the astute English sportsman and financier. In the interim, unbeknownst to Ali, his people had been contacted by Mobutu Sese Seko, president of Zaire, to have Ali return to his country at the same time as the invited guest. Quite an honor, but jt meant that Jarvis was left hanging, exposed to all types of character assassination in the press. He had, after all, advertised Ali, and now either he produced Ali, or lost face. Jarvis decided to see if he could do something about it with Ali as he came through Paris. He met the plane, and Ali was very happy to see Jarvis, and invited him into his limo for the ride into Paris. Bula, the Zaire minister, refused to have Jarvis accompany them in the limo. Ali not only insisted, but made Bula ride in the jump seat. Jarvis then explained the predicament that Ali had placed him in, and produced the ads and pamphlets to illustrate his point. Ali saw his duty and did not hesitate for a second, turning to Bula and telling him he was simply going to comply with a previous commitment, and that though he was extremely sorry, the president would just have to wait. Right is right in Ali's mind.

Ali is a very generous man. Before he is through, he will have given away millions of dollars to needy and not-so-needy people. Our camp is a prime example of wasteful generosity, for as in many things regarding charity, the brassy are the recipients, not the needy. The needy are back home, too weak and shameful to ask. The strong, the con artist, the shameless are up front asking for, and getting, the lion's share of the dole. Unfortunately, because Ali is a primary thinker, he's likely to give to the one who is immediately in front of him asking. During the second Frazier fight in New York, we were staying across the street in a hotel and had to cross the street to the Garden three times: to the weigh-in, back from the weigh-in, and back for the fight. Those three trips cost Ali about $5,000. Incredible, isn't it? How did that happen? Angelo carries some money, or his brother Jimmy does, and we all push through a crowd, most of whom are asking for tickets. Ali pauses and asks Angelo if he has any hundred-dollar tickets left. No, says Angelo, knowing he has better uses for any tickets he may happen to have than to dole them out to moochers. Let them buy tickets at the box office.

So Ali starts handing out money! Is this possible, or am I making this up? Doesn't it have a bizarre quality? The first street crossing is tough but now the word is out that Ali will fall for a story, and the New York professionals come running. The trip back across is a scene from a Fellini movie. Every type of junkie, wino, cripple, and beggar stands in our way, and Ali hands out the bills to his public. When are they ever going to get a chance to see Ali fight in person again? I am thinking that the only way these guys are going to see Ali is in the hallucinations that this windfall is going to buy for them through drink and/or drugs. Nonetheless, I have seen Ali hand out real cash to any and every type, including redneck crackers who are insulting him because they lost money on a bet. He gives them back their money, saying, "Now don't be mad at me." On the other hand, I have seen him cut the salaries of the fight camp for no reason at all. That's one of the incongruities that makes up the Ali enigma. He does not sling money around the camp when he makes a five-million-dollar touch, because he says the Internal Revenue will not allow it. I will say he pays most of his people ten times what is normally paid in boxing, so I cannot criticize him for that.

Ali is a very loving man. Ali loves the human race. The smaller the person the better he likes him, although he is impressed with external signs of wealth and position. He cannot accept the fact that I am financially solvent, because he has seen my ghetto office where I do a lot of free work. A while back he was contemplating selling me his Rolls as a method of paying me for my donated services (before they began to equate trustworthiness with cash), but the price was around $19,000 and he could not bring himself to accept the fact that I was able to pay him, thinking I would have to go to a bank and put myself in hock to buy the car. (I never did buy it.) He has a spectacular record of aid to his family and friends. He has no enemies. He loves to shower unexpected affection and help on unsuspecting strangers. His reward is the look of amazement on the face of the recipient. He will stop on a wet rainy day on an expressway to help a trucker change a tire without introducing himself, and revel in the reaction when his identity is revealed.

Is Ali a truly funny man? My god, yes! Although, as I said, he is often driven to stereotyped drivel simply to handle the onslaught of humanity he has to deal with, he is a truly funny man in his day-to-day life. Ali came to my house unannounced one day, and went through the kitchen. Now I have a Cuban refugee maid, about 55 years old, who must be the only person in the world who does not know Muhammad Ali, and here she turns around and finds Ali, a gigantic six-foot-three-inch black male in her kitchen, and it is dark outside. She hurries to my room and tells me about a huge black man in her kitchen. By the description I know it is Ali, so I dress and step down to see him. He loves cars and has come by to see an old Packard convertible I have in the garage. I know he loves the Rolls, so I drive him to a neighbor's house.

My neighbor is a young kid who was left a lot of money by his family, and he has taken to importing old Rolls Royces from England. I live in a very tidy, exclusive residential section, but his house stands out from the rest because it is downright shabby. His yard is littered with oil patches and hubcaps, but spread along the front and side of the house are thirteen Rolls Royces.

Ali regards the shabby house and the profusion of wildly expensive Rolls, shakes his head, and says, "A *nigger* must live here, Doc. Only a *nigger* can have a house as ratty as this with all these expensive cars in front of it."

Finally all of these qualities are wrapped up in an attractive package. Ali physically is a very impressive man. He is huge. He is very physical. He hugs both men and women easily. He has a soft handshake, as do most fighters for some reason, but a bear-like hug. He does have a quick temper, but it seldom gets a chance to show itself to the outside world because not too many people cross him, and because he genuinely dislikes arguments of all types. His temper and the arguments come up chiefly with his family and, quite correctly, are his business and his alone. A lot of fuss was made over his arguments with Belinda, his mother, his father, and his brother in Manila, but Ali emerges the winner, and he's usually right in what he maintains. He is the one that holds his families together, and he asks for freedom from embarrassment from them. When they embarrass him he reacts by getting mad, and his remarks can be cutting, but, characteristically, he ends up atoning for the hurt he inflicts. He is a strong family man. He is a male supremacist. He is the *boss*. He has a very strong character that *none* can tame or tell what to do. He is in total command of himself. Liston was a very strong man, but a pussycat in the hands of his wife Geraldine.

On any scale you wish to evaluate Ali as a human being, you would have to rate him an exceptional person. He is a winner, in the ring and out. He has a strong attractive personality, is generous and loving, has no hidden mean streak, is given basically to giving rather than receiving. Physically, I don't know a more perfect human being. Emotionally, he is an integrated, useful, diverse personality. If he is not an intellectual giant, he is at least the smartest in his field, and there is nothing wrong with his street smarts.

I have been exposed to sides of Ali that no one has seen except his family and closest associates, and the biggest surprise I got from him was the wonderful way he accepts adversity, whether a loss in the ring, a physical setback, like the broken jaw, or an emotional shock like a divorce. He is an exceptional person, and if writers find him hard to figure out,

welcome to the club. But I respectfully submit that it is difficult to know anyone in one or two weeks, and that is what
writers are forever trying to do.

In closing, I would like to say that in my varied career I
consider my Ali years as a stunning highlight in my life.

The night Ali won back the title in Africa, after all the
years of struggle, was a high I could not hope to reproduce in
my lifetime. It has been a privilege and a joy to be part of the
Ali Circus. I will not see its like again.